Siô N

SEVEN
THAT'S I

Tracy Hansen live
editor of the *Catho
translator for two
June 1990, she has been writing articles ior uic
religious press about her experience of facing up
to childhood sexual abuse.

HAT

ONE for sorrow,
TWO for joy,
THREE for a wedding,
FOUR for a boy,
FIVE for silver,
SIX for gold,
SEVEN for a secret that's never been told!

CHILDREN'S RHYME

'You will be sorrowful,
but your sorrow will turn to joy.'

(John 16:20)

SEVEN FOR A SECRET THAT'S NEVER BEEN TOLD

Healing the wounds of sexual abuse in childhood

.U

TRACY HANSEN

TRi△NglE

First published 1991
Triangle
SPCK
Holy Trinity Church
Marylebone Road
London NW1 4DU

British Library Cataloguing in Publication Data

Hansen, Tracy
Seven for a secret that's never been told.
1. Children. Sexual abuse. Pastoral work
I. Title
248.86

ISBN 0-281-04540-2

Typeset by Inforum Typesetting, Portsmouth
Printed in Great Britain by
Courier International, East Kilbride

CONTENTS

For Pearl
and the children of tomorrow

ACKNOWLEDGEMENTS

My special thanks go to those who have been with me, and stayed with me, throughout these years of trauma. Without them, there would be no story to tell. Their unfailing kindness and everlasting patience, even when I was at my most hostile and defensive, have taught me to believe in myself again and given me the courage to face a new future. And it is a *new* future, for, because of them, this is a story of hope and healing.

My thanks go too to the many people who have helped without knowing it, simply by being themselves. Their company and friendship have helped me through many a dark moment and shown me that life is worth living.

In the preparation of this book, the contribution of my friends Sue Farrant and Kevin O'Connell has been invaluable. Their honest and constructive criticism and support added much of value to my original draft, and persuaded me that my story was worth sharing.

Finally, I would like to thank Philip Law, my editor at SPCK, whose encouragement and consideration brought the project to completion.

For any errors or omissions I alone am responsible.

PREFACE

In the last few years, the previously taboo subject of the sexual abuse of children has come out into the open. Extensive media coverage has brought it into the public eye and increased our awareness of the nature and extent of the problem, and the plight of the child victims. Efforts are being made to provide help and support for children who have been, or are being, sexually abused.

But while awareness of child sexual abuse is new, the problem itself is not. There are many victims who have now grown up, and the new openness and acceptance of the subject is causing some of them to come forward, looking for the help they need which was not available when they were children. Child sexual abuse has severe long-term effects which do not heal naturally, and these adults, the children of yesterday, continue to suffer as a result of sexual abuse that may have happened decades before.

I am one of the children of yesterday who was abused more than a quarter of a century ago, and this is my story of the road towards recovery. As a Catholic, I chose to approach the Church for help, and was fortunate in finding people whose sensitivity, insight and compassion enabled me to set out on my journey of healing. They include priests, religious and lay people, and though none had had experience in helping adult survivors of child sexual abuse, they were able to provide me with the help and support I needed.

However, the Church has, as yet, no pastoral approach for people like me. The existence of this problem area has recently been recognised by the Catholic

Bishops' Conference, and a response to it is beginning. There is recognition that this is an area with special pastoral needs, and that priests and others who may find themselves in the front line for disclosures of past sexual abuse need to be trained to handle such disclosures with tact and sensitivity.

Even with the best of intentions, someone faced with a disclosure of sexual abuse that happened many years previously may say or do things that make the situation worse. This seems to arise mainly from ignorance of what is involved as an adult starts to face up to the past for the first time. There is an urgent and pressing need for some basic training to be provided for, with the subject increasingly being talked about and reported, many more adults find themselves unable to shut out their past any longer.

Aware of this void, I began to write articles in the religious press in June 1990. I hoped that by sharing my own experience and by saying what had and had not helped me, I could help to equip people a little better in handling such cases. I have had some bad experiences (though fortunately they were rare) from which I was able to learn how a dismissive or intrusive comment can have a devastating and disproportionate effect. And from many good experiences, I know how a kind word or genuine expression of understanding and concern can also have a disproportionate effect in diminishing the pain and sense of isolation.

The response to my articles has been overwhelming. There is a readiness, willingness and even eagerness on the part of many people to learn how to help, how to suport and how to avoid pitfalls. Once told that something they are doing is unhelpful, many instantly change; no one could ask for more than that.

The discovery that there are so many people of good-will who are willing to share the trauma of past sexual abuse has been one of the greatest joys of my journey.

For them, for other victims like myself and for those who simply want to know more, this is my story of some of the ways and means I found through which I was able to reclaim my past and begin to come to terms with it.

INTRODUCTION

The Secret

The 'secret that had never been told' was one that I had kept, even from myself, for almost the whole of my life. But the time came one Thursday afternoon four years ago, shortly after my forty-first birthday, when I found I could keep it no longer. After six weeks of panic attacks, disturbed sleep, and symptoms very like a bad bout of flu, a memory gently edged its way back into my tired and distracted mind. On the radio, in my half-asleep state, I heard someone say, 'But he wasn't a stranger', and I heard myself thinking, in response, 'No, he wasn't, and that was the problem.'

And then it was there, the memory I had succeeded so well in denying for so long: I had been raped by a man I knew well, a friend of my family and occasional babysitter, whom we had all liked and trusted. I had been under seven, and it had shattered my entire world. It had seemed like a nightmare, too terrible to be real, and totally unlike anything else I had ever known. I had no words for it; I did not understand. Yet I had a deep sense of shame and wrongdoing. I knew intuitively that I had been involved in something terribly wrong, something I did not want anyone else to know about. After all, I was the one who had asked if I could go with him when he said he was going to pick blackberries.

He took me home some time later where, to my surprise, I found that life was going on as normal, just as it always had. No one noticed that anything was wrong with me: I couldn't believe it. How could they not notice? Yet they didn't, and the routine of normal life came and enveloped me.

The rapist had made me promise to keep silent. He threatened terrible things if I ever told anyone what had happened, and he made me feel responsible and guilty about what he had done. But a little later, I decided I had to break that promise. My rudimentary sexual knowledge had led me to the conclusion that I would now have a baby. Obviously my mother had to be told, if only for the simple reason that she would have to get back the cot and highchair she had recently given away.

Despite my lack of vocabulary, she understood the implication of what I said – and she did not believe me. It never occurred to her, I think, that I might be telling the truth, for this was at a time when the whole subject of sexual abuse was taboo: it simply 'didn't happen'; or if it did, it didn't happen to people like 'us'. And so she turned on me and told me that that was a terrible thing to say, and I must never say anything like that about anyone ever again. And to impress upon me the serious-ness of making up such stories, I was punished.

My world fell apart a second time. I had been told, in effect, that it had not happened. Could I be right and all of them wrong? The nightmarish quality of the rape itself, added to this, seemed to question the reality of what had happened.

I never spoke of it again, not for over thirty years. I pushed it right out of my conscious mind and refused to think about it. I tried to carry on as normal, but life had lost all its vitality. It became a struggle simply to survive. Sometimes, as I grew up and life was really difficult, or if I was very unhappy for some reason, I would remem-ber in a panic that there was something I must be sure to forget. I would go down deep inside myself to make sure I had really forgotten and was in no danger of remembering. I would find that it was down there, sealed off with 'barriers' that prevented me from remembering what was contained within it, and that reassured me.

Unlike other painful childhood experiences, the effects of the rape did not heal naturally as I grew up. Although the memory was so deeply buried that I rarely even dreamt of anything connected with the rape, it exerted a negative influence on the whole of my life as I became an adolescent and then an adult. I suffered from anxiety and depression, and these became a backdrop to my life, creating a greyness in which I was continually trapped. I suffered from sleeping and eating disorders, and various psychosomatic complaints, particularly of a gynaecological nature, for which years of testing and minor operations could find no organic cause. I found it difficult to form relationships with other people, both men and women, and none lasted for more than a few years. At times, I felt suicidal.

When the memory returned, very gently, my initial feeling was one of relief and release: so that was what it was; that was what had gone wrong almost at the beginning of my life; of course – I had always known, in a way.

But this sense of peace and wellbeing did not last long. Buried with my memory were all the violent feelings associated with it, which I had never allowed myself to feel. There were anger, terror, hatred, grief, shame, bitterness, rage and searing emotional pain. These sprang up into the present with all the freshness and spontaneity of a child's feelings. They totally overwhelmed me and made it impossible for me to sleep, eat or work. I was submerged in what I would later realise was delayed rape trauma. For more than thirty years, these feelings had been bottled up, and the effort of

3

keeping them down had sapped my energy and vitality all my life.

I could not cope with this alone. But where was help to be found? I had never heard of a problem like this before. I desperately wanted to be able to tell someone, to have someone with whom I could talk about it, but I was terrified of doing so. I was afraid I would not be believed, for I had trouble believing it myself and at times it seemed as if it must be just a terrible nightmare. I was afraid that I might be told that I should not be worrying about it now since it all happened a very long time ago. And I was afraid that I would be blamed for it, since I felt that I must somehow be responsible for it happening.

More than ten years before, I had entered the Roman Catholic Church. At the time the rape took place, I had been attending a Catholic primary school, even though my family was not Catholic. The burden of the rape that I was carrying, and my deep sense of guilt and shame, caused me, some weeks after the rape, to approach my teacher. 'Sister,' I asked, after the rest of my class had gone outside for break, 'is there anything so terrible or so bad that God can't forgive it?' 'No, dear,' she replied in a matter-of-fact tone, 'nothing at all. And don't ever let anyone tell you anything different.' I skipped out to join the others in the playground. These people understood these things! They understood about sin and darkness, and perhaps they would even understand about rape. That was my first glimpse of hope, for on that day I began to believe that one day it might be possible to find help.

Those encouraging words from my teacher stayed with me, and were instrumental in my decision to enter the Catholic Church over twenty years later. And so, when my memory returned, I believe they also played a part in my decision that it was to the Church that I would turn for help.

There was a priest whom I knew well, and whom I had grown to trust. That trust had been built up over several years, for I did not find it easy to trust people: someone I had once trusted and felt safe with had turned on me, and I expected that to happen again. I always expected it to happen in any relationship, and it was a kind of self-fulfilling prophecy. Every relationship I had, had broken down, largely because I expected it to.

Nevertheless, I went to him. Desperation led me to take that risk, and many others later. I had nothing to lose, not even my self-respect, for I had none. I told him, and I was believed. The kindness and gentleness with which he accepted my story gave me the strength and courage to start to face up to the past. I had the one indispensable aid I needed: I had a friend.

Soon afterwards, and for various different reasons, I told other people as well. Usually it was because I was looking for help of a particular kind, which I felt that person might be able to give. Before long, I found I was surrounded by a network of people who were willing to stay with me and help as they could.

However, we were facing a vast, uncharted land. None of them knew much about child sexual abuse or how to help an adult who was trying to work through it. My life, as the trauma broke and continued for over three years, was like the area of devastation left behind after a nuclear bomb has gone off. There were no paths through this wasteland; I had to find my own, with the help and support of these friends.

I believed, with certainty, that it was through the Gospel that I would find what I needed. It seemed to me that a problem of the magnitude I was facing was something that only God could heal. No area of my life had been left unaffected by the rape: the healing I was looking for, and hoping for, had to be radical. As radical as the bringing of a new life out of death. As radical as resurrection. I decided that I had to find out whether what the Gospel promised was true.

I was entering the area of mystery: the mysteries of evil and suffering, and the mysteries of healing and love of which the Gospel speaks. Mystery lies at the heart of the Christian faith: we speak of the mysteries of the incarnation and redemption, and the mystery of God himself. Mystery is something that human intelligence can only ever grasp partially: whatever understanding we have of it at any one time is always capable of fuller and deeper development. A mystery is never exhausted: it is always possible to go further into it.

The language of mystery is the language of symbols. Christian prayer and liturgy are full of symbols: the water used in baptism, bread and wine used in the Eucharist, the chrism used for confirmation. As well as tangible, physical symbols, there are verbal symbols of metaphors and stories, and pictorial symbols as well. A symbol, in the true sense, is not merely a sign: it does not only point to another, invisible reality beyond itself, but participates in it and enables us to interact with it.

Symbols speak to the deepest level of our being, levels that words and arguments alone cannot reach. They speak to the level where we ourselves are mystery – the mystery of our being and our uniqueness, and the mystery of our relationship with God. They have a power to heal, for the word 'symbolic' derives from Greek roots originally, and means 'to draw together, to make whole'. Its opposite is 'diabolic' meaning 'to cause to fall apart, disintegrate'.

I was not brought up or educated in the language of

symbols. I was far more familiar with rational reasoning and analysis as methods of understanding the world around me. But in facing up to the rape, I quickly found that this language, while useful at times, was inadequate. I had to learn the language of creative symbolism and imagination through which I could come to grips with my experience in the deepest possible way, and thus enter into the mystery of healing.

This is a book about healing, about travelling through a wasteland and encountering conflicts and issues within myself that could only be reached in 'symbolic' ways, for the wounds created by child rape reach down to the depths of my being. I had to be inventive, creative and imaginative in finding methods that would work for me.

Each of the sections that follows describes one of those methods. I try to explain what I did, why I did it, and what the outcome was. Since they worked for me, it is my hope that they may also work, in some form, for others as well, and that other victims, or those helping them, will be able to adapt or translate them to their own specific circumstances and needs. Or perhaps, simply looking at the range of activities presented here, they will be able to find new methods of their own, using different methods and forms of symbolic play.

One of the ways that children appropriate and grasp the meaning of their experiences is through play. Within each adult survivor of child sexual abuse, there is the child she once was, a wounded child who has not yet been able to express her feelings and understand what has happened to her. The activities suggested in this book are mainly for that child. They are means of self-expression, methods of communication between the 'child within' and the adult that child has become, between the adult and other people, and between the victim and God.

STEPPING OUT

A Fairy Tale

This first activity is a creative re-expression of what happened to me, in the form of a fairy tale. As an adult looking back to my childhood from a distance of more than thirty years, I could remember very clearly what had happened, but I did not know how I had understood it as a child. What did the 'child-within-me' think had happened to her? Both the word and concept of rape had been unknown to me at that time. This exercise helped me, as an adult, develop a fuller appreciation of the child's point of view. One of the things that surprised me about this story after I had written it is that it contains no overt sexual imagery. Instead, it tells me that as a child I had understood the rape more in terms of an act of aggression that left me maimed.

The story tells how I set out on the journey of healing, for I am the bear who is the main character. In a language that children would understand, it describes my first steps out of the world of fear and isolation in which I had spent most of my life. First, I had to believe that healing was possible, even if others did not. In the story, it is an encounter with Bee 4 that reveals that it is. Bee 4 is 'before', the recognition that life had not always been like this: there had been a time, before the rape, when I was a normal, happy, secure child. Then, like the bear, I had to set off on a difficult journey on my own, even though I did not know how to get to where I was going. Next, I had to overcome my belief that I was 'bad' or 'wicked'. That

8

happened through an encounter with another person, described in the story as the 'plush otter'. Only then was I ready to begin 'the long walk out of the forest and the woods', which was the start of the journey towards wholeness.

The experience does not necessarily have to be told in the form of a fairy tale: that is simply the form that appealed to me. But other possibilities could include telling it as a horror story, an episode in a soap opera, a Shakespearean tragedy, a Monty Python sketch, and so on. The purpose is to make contact with the child's mentality and find some way to express it.

The Great Bear who lived in the sky had been worried for years because when he looked down at night he saw children crying in their beds. He wanted to do something about it, but since he was unable to leave the sky (for the Great Bear is made of stars and can't live anywhere except the sky) he worried and worried about it for a very long time before he thought of what he could do. One night, he took a little cloud that was tinted gold by the setting sun, and shaped it in his starry paws, and it became a little plush teddy bear. He held the little bear close against his heart; the bear hiccupped, and then he sneezed. 'Bless you,' said the Great Bear, and gave him a hanky. The Great Bear explained what the little bear was to do, and put him on the top of a moonbeam. The little bear slid all the way down and landed, BUMP, in the bed of a child who had been crying in the dark for many nights. The child was very surprised. The little bear stood up, rather shakily, and bowed, just as the Great Bear had told him. 'How do you do?' he said politely. 'I am your bear.' And the child laughed.

That child never cried in the dark again because he had his bear for company, and the Great Bear was so pleased by the success of his plan that he made thousands and thousands of little bears so that every child could have one. The bears not only kept their children company, but they told them wonderful stories that explained the Meaning of Everything, and the children listened and learned a lot of new things.

At first, parents were very pleased about the arrival of bears – no more trailing up the stairs in the middle of a good radio play because a child was crying for no reason. No more wondering how to entertain the children on wet afternoons, because bears seemed to have an endless store of ideas for Things To Do. Of course, the parents didn't know it was bears' doing, for the bears looked just like the other stuffed animals the children had. In fact, the Great Bear had been careful to make sure he put labels on the little bears saying, 'Made in Hong Kong' or something similar so that no one except the children knew there was anything special about them.

Things had been going very well for quite a few years, but then people started to notice that something was happening to their children. They weren't growing up like their parents. They didn't think it was important to make lots of money or be successful at something – they thought it was far more important to play. Even when they grew up, they played. They laughed a lot, which couldn't be right, for grown-ups don't laugh much, and never worried about where lunch was coming from. Parents tried to tell them that they would have to worry about where lunch was coming from or there might not be any, but they didn't, and lunch always came from somewhere nonetheless.

It didn't take people very long to realise that something had to be done. You couldn't have a generation of children growing up who refused to worry about lunch, or supper. Why, the next thing would be that they'd refuse to worry about really important things like mortgages and life insurance, and then where would the world be? So a special team set about investigating the problem and finding out where the trouble was coming from. They set up children into 'control groups' and experimented. It didn't take them long to find out that children who were deprived of their plush animals soon started to worry about where lunch was coming from, and showed every sign of becoming neurotic about mortgages in later life. So the answer was simple – get rid of all the plush animals.

The government (which is a collection of a lot of parents) ordered a Purge. There were too many plush animals to be exterminated, so they were driven out instead. Purge Police roamed the streets, netting and catching every plush animal they saw. They went into children's playrooms and bedrooms rounding them all up and, using Plush Detectors, they even found the hiding places where children had pushed them. The children cried, of course, which parents took to be a good sign. They said things like 'It's for your own good', and 'Don't be such a cry-baby. You're supposed to be a big boy', and so on. And soon the world was full of children crying at night again, but their bears were not there to help them.

Child psychiatrists were invented, and parenting seminars, but the children didn't respond, and were labelled 'ungrateful wretches'. They cried in the dark again, remembering their lost bears.

The Purge Police took cartloads of plush animals deep into a forest where they would get lost. Bears have never had a very good sense of direction when they can't see the Great Bear and get their bearings, and in the forest, since the branches were thick over their heads, they didn't know how to get back. Most of them tried, but they got even more lost than before.

Life became very difficult for the plush animals. They lived in small groups in caves or burrows by the roots of big trees. Their plush got bedraggled and matted. They had to spend all day every day searching for things to eat, like blackberries and windfall apples. Several of them died from eating deadly nightshade before word got around that not everything that looked good to eat really was. They got very cold at night, too, because they were used to being in warm beds. And they missed their children terribly.

Well, they got used to it, and developed a life of a sort, and found that if plush animals worked together, they could build better shelters and find food more easily, and at night they sat round fires and made up very sad songs about their children and the games they had known.

This had been going on for quite a time, and there was even a study group looking for Ways Out and places where they could see the Great Bear and so find their way home. There were groups out scouting, and some of them reported that the trees got thinner if you went far enough, though others said they didn't really, it was just because the leaves had started to drop off. One of the bears, who was a bit of a philosopher, had a plan for climbing up trees, and was sure that if he got high enough, he could grab the Great Bear's tail and make him notice. In fact, things were really starting to look a little hopeful again when the Fierce Animals came.

They were black and sleek, with names like Stoat and Ferret, and they looked like the Purge Police. The plush animals shrieked and ran, but there were too many of the Fierce Animals and they moved much faster, and before long, they'd herded them all into a large pen surrounded by barbed wire. They left them there without food for quite a time while they lolled around playing cards and laughing with a nasty, sharp sort of laugh.

Eventually, Stoat got up and stretched and said, 'OK, you animals, it's time to be going.'

'Where to?' asked a young lop-eared rabbit, timidly.

'Why the Punishment block, of course,' Stoat replied. 'We've heard from the People that you've been subverting their children. That's why they drove you out. Well, now you're going to be punished.'

'But we like children!' said a Mole, dolefully.

'You're very wicked animals, but you don't know it. You don't know that what you've been doing to the children is evil and wrong. Children are *supposed* to

13

grow up like their parents. They always have, and they always will. But you animals want to stop that happening. Well, that's evil.'

'It's not!' said a very brave mouse. 'Children like us!'

'Of course they do,' said Stoat. 'That's the whole point. But parents have got to protect their children from evil influences like you. Now, how many of you will admit that what you've been doing is wicked? Put up your paws, and let's see.'

Not a single plush animal put up his paw, but mostly it was because they were so confused by Stoat's argument that they no longer knew what to think.

'There!' said Stoat, triumphantly. 'You see? You don't know that you're wicked.' And the Fierce Animals lined the plush animals up for a march through the forest.

After three days, they were told to sit down and wait at the edge of a clearing. Then Stoat and a couple of other Fierce Animals went off and dragged in a huge block of wood with a white line painted on it.

'What's that?' whispered a plush monkey.

'The Punishment block', said Ferret, sneering.

It was a dreadful scene, as you can imagine. One by one the little plush animals were taken up to the block. They were asked if they knew yet that they were wicked, and when each one shook his head, Stoat shouted out 'Ear', or 'Left Paw', or 'Tail' or 'Nose', and the animal was led to the block, and that bit of him was chopped off.

There was a bear who tried to be very brave. Stoat had said 'Left Paw' when it was his turn, so he said goodbye to his paw as he stretched it out on the block. 'Perhaps they want bear-paw soup', he said to himself. 'I'll pretend I'm *giving* them my paw for bear-paw soup.' It didn't help very much, and when the axe fell

14

on his paw, he almost fainted from the effort of not crying. He had time to see that they didn't want his paw – they only threw it away, and that made him sadder than anything.

After the Punishment, the little animals were released, and went back to their homes in the forest. They were crying, and didn't know what to do. They tried to look after each other and care for their wounds, but the mouse died that same night, and over the next weeks, several others died as well, from festering wounds, or grief. The ones that survived grew thick scar tissue over their wounds, and stopped bleeding. They tried to live as they had before, but they were very frightened in case the Fierce Animals came back and chopped more bits off them.

The bears kept to themselves after that, and didn't mix with the other plush animals often. It was a long time before any of them admitted to each other why. But eventually, a grey bear said,

'It's because of us, isn't it?'

'What?' said a brown bear, as if he didn't know.

'That the other plush animals got bits chopped off them. It's bears that are doing what the parents don't like, not the other animals.'

There was a horribly long pause.

'Yes, it is our fault,' said an older bear. 'If it wasn't for us, none of this would've happened.'

'So we are wicked, then. The Fierce Animals were right.'

'Yes,' said a yellow bear, feeling the place where his ears had been. 'We are wicked. We just didn't know. And all those other animals have suffered because of us.'

'I never intended to hurt my child,' a white bear said, sadly.

15

'Nor me,' agreed the brown bear. 'I didn't know THEN that I was.'

'None of us knew. We didn't know we were wicked.'

'But we do now, and if we should ever doubt it, we have only to look at the other animals.'

'Oh, it's dreadful!' a pink bear said, hysterically. 'Have you seen the Mole? Both his front paws were cut off. He can't dig.'

'I don't know about all of you,' the brown bear said, 'but now I know that I'm wicked, I'm not going to try and get back to my child any more. He's better off without me. I never wanted to hurt him, and I still don't.'

'Nor me. I'm not going to try either.'

'Nor me.'

'Or me.'

'Or me.'

They were all agreed. They would stay in the forest and never try to find their children again.

It might have gone on like that forever if the bears hadn't started to run out of food. None of them had been very hungry since the Punishment, so they hadn't eaten much and the few berries that grew round about had been enough for them. But once they'd decided to stay where they were, and started to fit out bear pits and caves, they began to feel a little hungrier.

'We'll have to scout round and see what else there is,' they decided. So several of them set off in different directions. The bear who had lost his left paw went east – at least, he thought it was east. He knew east was where the sun was, so he walked towards it, but he'd sometimes find, at the end of a day, that he'd been right round in a circle. It was at the end of one of these circling days that the bear was sitting down under a tree when he thought he heard the Fierce Animals. He

16

didn't like heights, but quick as a flash, he climbed up the tree and hid in the branches.

'It's all right,' said a passing bee. 'It's only thunder.'

'Are you sure?' asked the bear, clinging on to his branch.

'Quite sure. Bees know everything that goes on. What are you doing here anyway? There aren't usually bears in this part of the forest.'

'Looking for food. We're all rather hungry. You know what happened to us, I suppose, if you know everything.

'We certainly do,' said the bee. 'Your poor paw. Look at it. Isn't it a shame.'

'Don't look at it!' the bear said. 'It's bad enough that it happened without anyone looking at it.'

The bee was a little sorry that he'd been tactless. 'Look,' he said, 'if you go up another couple of branches, you'll find our nest. Tell them I sent you, and they'll give you a honeycomb. My name's Bee 4.'

Sure enough, the nest was there. 'Bee 4 sent me,' the bear said.

'Ah, it'll be for a honeycomb then. How much do you want?'

'Lots,' said the bear.

'Right you are,' said the bees. 'Oh, look at your poor paw!'

'Don't!' said the bear.

'Why not?' said the bees. 'Here, lads, over here. Come and see this poor bear's poor paw!'

Bees circled all round him, murmuring sympathetically, and the bear got very embarrassed. To change the subject, he said, 'Where do you get your honey from?'

'Oh, a long way off,' said the bees. 'We make it from flowers that grow in a meadow.'

'I was over there yesterday,' Bee 9 said. 'You know what I heard? That there's someone who lives there

17

who mends plush animals. Why don't you go and get mended, bear?'

'I've got to get back,' the bear said. 'The others are hungry too. Thank you for the honey. It's very kind of you.'

So he took the honey and went home.

None of the other bears had found anything much that day, so they shared out the honeycomb among them. As the bear was eating it with the others, he could almost see the meadow the bees had spoken of – the place where flowers grew from which the bees made their honey – the place where . . . no, he wouldn't think of that. It couldn't possibly be true. Perhaps it was because he was so hungry that every time he took another bite of the honeycomb, the meadow got clearer and clearer in his mind.

It was a lovely place, on a slight hill, with grass that waved in the breeze and glistened in the sun. The flowers the bees used were pink, blue and white, and grew in the grass and the hedges. There were yellow ones, too, down by a stream, and just a few trees for shade. . . .

And someone lived there . . . no, that couldn't be right. That would be Too Good to be True.

Suddenly, the bear stopped musing, because he realised that all the others had stopped eating and were staring at him. He looked at their faces, all turned towards him, and was opening his mouth to ask what was the matter, when the yellow bear said, in an incredulous tone:

'THE BEES SAID *WHAT*?'

The bear realised that he must have said it. He hadn't meant to. It wouldn't be fair to get their hopes up. But,

'THE BEES SAID *WHAT*?' the yellow bear repeated.

'That there's someone in the meadow who can mend plush animals. Then he said, "Why don't you go and get mended, bear?" '

There was a long, stunned pause. Then the grey bear said, with a sigh,

'If only it was as simple as that!'

The other bears seemed almost relieved. 'Yes, if only it was as simple as that.'

'Don't you want to go and see?' the bear asked, confused.

'Fool's errand,' the blue bear said. 'They just want you to go off on a wild quest, and then they'll all buzz about laughing.'

'And besides,' a small beige bear chipped in, 'we're wicked, and that's why . . . and remember the other plush animals. What happened to them was our fault. We don't deserve to be mended. Not now.'

'But bees know everything,' the bear said.

'They *think* they do,' said the philospher bear, 'but it only stands to reason that they couldn't possibly. Look at it this way: a Thought is big, but a bee is little. You couldn't get many Thoughts inside a bee, so they can't really know much.' (The philosopher bear had had several Thoughts in his life, so he knew they were big and a bit painful.)

The bear left the rest of his honey, and got down from the table where the others were all agreeing with each other, and disagreeing with the bees. They didn't notice him go. And they didn't notice him go off on his own on a long quest to find the meadow.

It took a long time. He kept getting lost, and got caught in brambles a lot. Then he fell in a muddy pool, but he found the meadow in the end.

It was a lovely place, exactly the way he'd imagined it. The sun was shining, the flowers were glowing, and the stream chuckled in the distance. The bear walked all around, but no one seemed to be there. A little disappointed, he went down to the stream and started trying to wash the mud off. He thought he heard a little splash, and looked up, but he couldn't see anything there. Then, after a moment, he realised that someone was watching him. There were two eyes looking out from the hedge, nice, kind-looking eyes.

The bear sat down, and was very quiet, and after a minute or two, the animal came out. It was a plush otter. They aren't very common, but the bear had met one or two, so he knew he had nothing to fear.

It took the bear a long time to get to know the otter. Sometimes he followed him, pretending he wasn't, that he was just going for a walk that way. Other times he sat and watched him play in the stream. It was a plush otter all right, a little animal like himself, but the otter didn't have any bits missing. The bear hid his paw behind his back.

Then, one day, the otter spoke to him: 'What's that behind your back?'

The bear wondered why he hadn't said 'Hello' first, or 'How do you do?' but perhaps otters didn't. He'd never known any really well.

'Just my paw,' he said, trying to sound nonchalant.

'Or your missing paw,' the otter said.

'Do you want to see it?' the bear asked, remembering the bees.

'Only if you want me to.'

Well, he decided he did, so he showed the otter his paw. The otter said, 'There's someone in the meadow who can mend you.'

The bear got up, and ran round and round and round the meadow looking. There was no one there. So he ran round and round and round the other way. But still there was no one there. Except the otter, of course!

The bear went back to the otter. 'Please will you mend my paw?'

'Are you a wicked bear?'

The bear felt sad. 'I must be,' he said. 'That's why they cut off my paw.'

'Am I a wicked otter?'

'No!' the bear said quickly. 'You're lovely. Best otter in the world. No one chopped bits off you, so you aren't wicked.'

'How do you know they didn't chop off my nose?'

'Because you've got a nose, silly otter!'

The otter patted the bear's bad paw, and said, 'Silly bear!'

Well, the bear asked the otter dozens of questions, and the otter didn't seem to mind. But whatever the bear asked him, the otter replied, 'Are you a wicked bear?'

'Did someone mend your nose?'

'Are you a wicked bear?'

'Did you live somewhere the Fierce Animals didn't find?'

'Are you a wicked bear?'

'Who is the one who can mend plush animals?'

'Are you a wicked bear?'

'Can plush animals who are wicked still be mended?'

'Are you a wicked bear?'

And so it went on, day after day, until the bear couldn't think of any more questions.

'Good,' said the otter. 'Now let's go and play.' So off they went to the stream.

The bear didn't know how to swim, so the otter showed him. The bear thought it was great fun, and learned to tumble in the water, just like the otter. While he was doing it one day, and they were both laughing a lot, the otter said again 'Are you a wicked bear?' The bear wasn't thinking, he was just having fun, so he said

'No, of course not. I'm a good bear.'

'That's right,' said the otter. 'Just look at your paw.'

He looked – and his lost paw was there! He turned it, he felt it, he opened and closed it – it was just as good as new!

'How?' said the bear.

'Aha!' said the otter, and sped away down the stream.

Bears aren't very good at Thinking Things Out, but he tried all the same. 'This is not my old paw. But it is my paw. But not my old paw. But a new paw, and it's mine. It's a Paw-Got-Back, not the paw thrown away. That means – it's an EVERLASTING paw! A paw that's got back will always be got back – so my paw is an everlasting paw!'

'That's right,' said the otter, who had come back by then. 'It's an everlasting paw. If you lose it again – but try not to – it will always be got back.'

'If they chop off my ears . . .'

'You can get everlasting ones.'

'If they chop off my nose . . .'

'You can get an everlasting one.'

'If they chop off my other paws . . .'

'You can get everlasting ones.'

They played this game for a long time. The bear said, 'Can all the plush animals be mended?'

'Of course,' said the otter. 'All you have to do is convince them that they're not wicked.'

'That won't be easy,' said the bear. 'They're sure, now, that they are.'

'Well,' said the otter, 'you can show them your paw. And there's something you can tell them, too.'

'What's that?' the bear asked.

'You can tell them, if you like, that they showed all along that they weren't wicked.'

'Did they?' said the bear.

'Yes, they did,' said the otter. 'When they thought

they were wicked, they decided to stay away from their children.'

'So?' said the bear.

'They didn't want to hurt them. That proves they aren't wicked, you see.'

The bear did see. Yes, he did see. Bears have never wanted anything but fun and happiness for their children, even if that meant staying away when they thought that bears might be wicked and bad for them.

'I'll come back,' said the bear.

'Yes, I know,' said the otter. 'You'll come back lots and lots, and we'll play. But now you're going. You have to tell all the others.'

'Yes,' the bear said. 'But I've got another question. Was it you or me who mended my paw?'

'Neither and both,' the otter said. 'This is a special place – perhaps you guessed. This is the meadow where, long ago, the First Bear played with his child. They're still here, in a way, though you can't see them, but it's a place where children and bears are safe. Safe for always. So when bears or children come here looking for something, they always find it. Always. You've found your paw, and you've found out, too, how to mend all the plush animals, which you wanted just as much.'

When the bear got back, some believed his story, and some didn't, but they all saw his paw. And they all realised that the otter had been right – they'd never been wicked at all.

The plush animals packed bags, and took down their shelters – 'We won't be wanting these again!' – and since the leaves had all dropped because winter had come, they could see the Great Bear if they tried. They all set out, that very same day, in twos and threes and fours, on the long walk out of the forest and the woods to find their children once more.

THE VOICE WITHIN

A Poem

Writing poetry, even if it is not particularly good poetry, can be a way of getting in touch with deeper levels. I find that rhyme and metre, even though these are unfashionable, are valuable aids in doing this. As I search for a rhyming word, it often seems to me that the 'right' one springs up from almost unconscious levels, and thus the process of writing a poem is like a dialogue with myself.

In the course of this dialogue, I often learn surprising things. For example, I have learned that there is a 'small, clear voice' within me, who is very unlike my normal self. It is someone who believes that life is good and worthwhile, whatever the pain, and above all it is someone who has hope. For many years, I did not know much about this person, but she is very like the child I once was, and I dared not listen too often or too closely for fear of what she might tell me.

But her message, through poems, is the Christmas message, 'tidings of comfort and joy'. Writing poems is a way I have found of letting her give it to me.

Life was like a perpetual winter in which the sun, a symbol of life and joy, was declining day by day. This went on for more than thirty years. Most of the time I was unaware that life could be any different, but occasionally, there was a spark of hope that someday things might be better. This poem came to me (I cannot honestly say that I wrote it in any deliberate sense) at a time when life was at a very low ebb. My memory of the rape was just beginning to stir, though all I felt was a sense of uneasiness, a feeling that something terrible had happened a long time ago. It took another four years for it to come to the surface.

Two parts of myself are in dialogue in this poem. The first two verses are a statement by my 'normal' self, reflecting a feeling of hopelessness and despair over the continual winter. Christmas was always a difficult time for me as a child. Many Christmas carols carried a message that made me feel like an outcast: 'Christian children all must be, Mild, obedient, good as he' said my favourite carol. Yet I was not 'good'. I had been contaminated by the rape. In a school nativity play, I was dressed in white and carried a candle in the final scene. I felt terrible about it – I had no right to be there with Mary, Joseph and Baby Jesus, no right to be there with the other children who were 'pure and holy' in a way that I could never be again. Yet I could not protest or say why I did not want to be in the play. Winter became most fully a time of desolation at Christmas as other people rejoiced over the birth of Christ.

Sometimes, though, at times like that something would break through from a deeper level, and that is the second speaker in the poem. Something would tell me that, if the Gospel was true, Christ had been born for me, for the outcasts, the abandoned, the rejected, and victims of sexual abuse, and that one day I might have more to rejoice about at Christmas than many others, even the angels, for 'they know not Christ as Saviour' as, perhaps, I would one day. If Jesus really did come for the sick, not the healthy, for the lost sheep and not the ninety-nine in the fold, for sinners and not for the righteous, then he came for me. This is what the second speaker believes, and so there is hope, however long the journey may be.

The pagans believed that when the sun reached its lowest ebb at the winter solstice, they must light bonfires to give it strength so that the days would grow longer again and the weather get warmer. That was the origin of the custom of the Yule log which would be burned as a sacrifice to the sun. The second speaker sees this as foreshadowing the birth of Christ, the True Sun, bringing the summer of eternal life that will never end.

Winter Solstice

'How can you cry, in coal-black December,
"Joy to the world!" The fire is an ember,
the sun's light is weakening, though I can remember
the bright days of June-time and noon-time;
   September,
the gold sheen and amber of flame-brazing rays.
But now, in the winter, the daylight is haze.

'How can you try, in white winter blinding,
to follow the strait path, winding and winding,
with never a beacon, never a signing,
all in the hope of a finding, a finding.
What could you find in some far cattle shed
to raise up the sun from its weak winter bed?'

'The journey I make is unending, and longer,
and yet with each step I grow stronger and
    stronger.
Stars are my beacon in clear winter skies,
snow is my sign-posting, masking disguise,
and showing the untrodden way. And my prize,
though newborn and swaddled and hidden in
    hay,
is light of the first fire, the uncreated day.
And surer than yule-fire, the Christchild's
    enduring
"Joy to the world" is the pale sun's refuelling.'

LOOKING BACK

A Short Story

There are objects in my past that, for one reason or another, I associate with the rape in some way. They are not necessarily things that existed at the time of the rape: they may have been earlier or later. But somehow they 'tell' me something about the person I was, or the way I coped, or the way I felt about myself and other people. As I grew up, I always felt that I was different from other children, contaminated or unclean in a way that they were not. I never felt as if I truly belonged anywhere.

There was a pink dress I had at school: by focussing on that pink dress, I was able to uncover and describe some of these unacknowledged feelings. It was in the process of doing that that I realised that one of my school friends had also been a victim of child sexual abuse. I had refused to recognise it at the time, for I had repressed all conscious memory of the rape, and so she frightened me in a way that I dared not acknowledge.

This short story is my way of explaining everything that pink dress stood for. It is a way, too, of telling 'Lindsay' that I finally understand.

There are other objects that I have used in this way: a table lamp that I associate with the dissolution of my world when my mother did not believe me; a chair that used to be in my bedroom and is linked with my undefined night terrors; a bottle of Yardley's lavender water that stood on my grandmother's dressing table, and is associated with the feeling of safety I had when I was in her house. I simply think about the object, and see what it will reveal.

The results of this kind of exercise do not have to be written down: the objects can simply be pondered slowly. But since some of the feelings produced may be strong or painful, it is a good idea to make sure, first, that there is someone to provide support.

Those in the sixth form would have a choice, the head-mistress announced during morning assembly. Instead of the navy blue gingham dresses the whole school had worn until then, the sixth formers would be given a choice of blue, yellow or pink.

This was the result of a previously unheard of process in our school. There had been a consultation of pupils and a vote to decide on a new summer uniform for the senior school. Consensus had been quickly reached on a plain, drip-dry fabric and a fashionable shirt-waister style, for this was in the 1960s, but the question of colour had proved problematic, and had resulted, finally, in the decision that there should be a choice of three harmonious shades.

I had not been included in the consultation since I was not expected to be among the group of fifth-formers who would be staying on into the sixth form. I had failed all my mock O levels, and that was taken to be an accurate assessment of my ability. In fact, in the third form, there had been talk of taking me away from the grammar school and sending me to the secondary modern. But I did reasonably well in the exams that year, and so I stayed.

Lindsay hadn't been consulted either. Like me, she was expected to leave at the end of the school year. She was a fair-haired little ghost with freckles who sat behind me in class. I was a dark-haired mouse who tended to arouse teachers' hostility because I often found it impossible to answer questions in class. We weren't exactly friends, Lindsay and I, but we weren't like the others, so we found ourselves together quite often. At least, we did for our first few years in the school, until Lindsay had her birthday party. It was the first party she had had, and it was the only time I ever went into her house.

There were ten of us there, all from the same class, and after the presents, games and birthday tea, we sat around the open fire roasting chestnuts. And then Lindsay's father came in. He was a tall, jovial, good-looking man, who dropped his briefcase on a chair in the hall and came to join us. 'Where's my birthday girl?' he called out. 'Come and give Daddy a big kiss.'

Poor Lindsay, I thought sympathetically, for my father often did that, too: spoke to me as if I was 5 not 15, and sometimes in front of my friends. I would blush and my toes would curl, and I'd send him a look of appeal that he never seemed able to decipher. I looked across at Lindsay, trying to convey a little shared understanding of the embarrassing habits of fathers. But Lindsay wasn't blushing. She had gone so white that her pale golden freckles stood out, solid and dark, on her translucent skin.

She walked like a robot across to her father, and stood there, passively waiting. My skin started to prickle as he kissed her cheek, and I noticed the not-quite-right movements of his hands. They were big, square-fingered hands, and they made me shudder. Then he slapped her bottom playfully: 'Come and introduce me to your little friends.'

We all stood up as they came towards us. 'This is Rosalie . . . Doreen . . . Marion . . . Celia . . .' He took each hand as it was offered, and bowed solemnly as he kissed it. They giggled, in turn, blushing, but after all, he was half-French.

As Lindsay turned towards me, my name on her tight lips, I suddenly felt as if I couldn't breathe. The room had become a scene in a film I was watching, but wasn't part of. My mouth went dry; I froze with fright as the man and his girl looked at me. Then, suddenly, I turned and fled – out of the door – past the briefcase on the

31

chair – up the softly-carpeted stairs. Where was the bathroom? The first door proved to be the airing cupboard, but the one next to it was right. Without even closing it behind me, I knelt down and was violently sick.

'Too much cake and excitement, I suspect,' Lindsay's father said when I returned. I nodded mutely, without raising my head, holding my glass of water so tightly that I feared it would crack. I stayed at the edge of the group as they sat on the hearthrug, hugging their knees, eagerly listening to the ghost stories he was telling from the depths of his armchair.

Lindsay was quite popular at school the next day. The girls all agreed that the ghost stories had been the best part. But I didn't join the chattering group, and got permission to stay inside, on my own, at break. I didn't want to be near Lindsay any more. She frightened me. She frightened me with what I knew.

Lindsay had a permanent dispensation from games because of her asthma. I used to get out of it as often as I could, forging notes from my mother, or always managing to have the wrong equipment. When I finally brought my hockey stick to school each year, the class had changed to tennis. My tennis racquet broke more strings than anyone else's, and my shirt was always at home for washing. So Lindsay and I had spent most of the games periods in companionable silence in the library.

But now I was faced with a dilemma. I no longer wanted to be in the library if Lindsay was there. Being near her meant being near my fear. But that meant I would have to do games.

I didn't mind the games themselves – it felt good to be out on the playing field, away from the concrete and glass enclosure of the school. I didn't mind running around with a hockey stick, though I usually tried to be a defender: they didn't get tackled so often, and were less likely suddenly to find themselves surrounded by a pressing crowd of other players. I quite liked my turn at the newly-introduced athletics. My time for the 100 yards was one of the best, and I was good at javelin, too. I would close my eyes and let my mind go blank, and a hidden well of anger would rise up and launch the javelin into the far horizon.

It was the changing rooms that were the horror: changing my clothes in front of other girls, listening to their comments about their own, and others', developing bodies, hearing their jokes and adolescent innuendoes. It made me feel cold and shaky, and trapped. And worst of all were the showers. I tried forgetting my towel, but I was handed a school one. I tried to catch a verruca by walking on tiles that a girl who was alleged to have one, undeclared, had just walked on. I volunteered to put the sports equipment away, and dawdled in the shed, hoping I'd be too late for a shower before the bell went. Sometimes it worked.

But Lindsay and I were still in the same class, as we always had been, and her desk was still right beind mine because her last name came after mine, alphabetically. I could hear her soft, asthmatic breathing: she was there, always there, right behind me.

I don't know if I grew to hate her or not. Perhaps it was myself I hated. Or perhaps I just hated the constant reminder behind me. By the time we entered the fifth form, I desperately wanted to get free, to get away from her, and everything she represented. If I did well, I might get moved up to the B stream. If I did badly, I would almost certainly get put down to the D stream. It was easier to do badly, and it took only one appalling term. But my parents intervened, saying that there had been difficulties at home, and that my grandmother had recently died. So I went back to the C stream and my desk in front of Linsday's.

I'll be leaving school, I thought, at the end of June. My parents had enrolled me in a secretarial college. While the other girls had charts to cross off the days until the summer holidays, I made one to cross off the days of seeing Lindsay. I taped it inside my desk lid, and used a special red biro to put a big X through each day. It wasn't long to wait: I could manage it if I knew the end was in sight.

My O level results came while we were on holiday. I hadn't cared about the exams at all. I didn't need any qualifications for the secretarial course, and so I hadn't bothered to work. I had done the papers, one after another, during a blisteringly hot two weeks in June. The humid gymnasium, where we sat at our numbered desks, spaced well apart to prevent cheating, rippled to the sounds of rustling paper and occasional sighs. Lindsay sat behind me, of course, except for geography, which she wasn't taking. I could still hear her breathing.

I dashed through the papers as fast as I could, scarcely reading the questions, and putting down whatever came into my head, frantic to get away, away from the exams, away from school, away from Lindsay – forever.

My aunt forwarded my results to the caravan where we were staying. My father handed me the envelope, his eyes bright with hope. For a moment, I wished that I had really tried, for his sake. He was the only person in the world who had gone on loving me, just as I was. But he didn't know. If he had known, he wouldn't have loved me any more, just as my mother didn't. She knew, though she didn't dare admit it, even to herself. She had called me a wicked, evil child for making up such a story about her friend.

Seven passes, with top grades. I'd only failed geography. My father hugged me and hugged me, gave me a £5 note, and rushed out to the phonebox. He came back radiant: it was all arranged. I could stay on at school and do A levels, and try for university entrance. I'd never seen him so excited or happy. 'Didn't I tell you, Mother? Haven't I always said she was bright? Just a late developer, that's all. Why, she can be anything she wants to be now!'

We went, Mother and I, to the school outfitters to buy material and a pattern for my sixth-form dress. Pale blue, yellow or pink. I stood in front of a full length mirror while Mother held fabric up against me. 'Not the yellow,' she said after a while, 'it makes you look pasty.' It was the pink that had taken my fancy, but I knew I had to go carefully. Mother still made most of my clothes, but she had never made anything pink, not since – well, not since I was nine and we moved away from there. But the deep, rose pink made me look alive. 'You can be anything you want to be now,' my father had said. Anything I wanted? I wanted to be alive again, as I had been as a little girl, in my pink frilly dresses, with my white hair ribbons.

In the mirror, I stopped seeing the thin, pale adolescent. I saw again the little girl I had once been, running, laughing, chattering, playing and wearing little pink dresses.

'The blue's nice,' I ventured, sure of my ground. She took the bait. 'But it's such an unattractive shade. I wonder why they couldn't have chosen something a little less dull.'

It was with mixed feelings that I returned to school a couple of weeks later. I'd hated it for five years, but my father's words still rang in my ears: 'Anything you want to be, anything at all.' And the sixth form would be different, freer, more grown up, like the dress. And there would be no Lindsay behind me any more, breathing.

A notice on the board told us to assemble in the hall. There was already a swirl of new, coloured dresses in there, all the girls chattering excitedly about holidays, boyfriends, the new teachers. It was a little while before I realised that no one else was wearing pink. Blue had captured 70% of the vote, and yellow took the remaining 30%. Pink wasn't even in the running. Not even Rosalie, whose pink nylon petticoat had once caused a scandal in the changing rooms, had chosen pink.

I stood there, more alone than I had ever been. My rose pink, the colour of life and hope, had betrayed me. It marked me out as different again, and exposed me to the world. Tears of disappointment and despair stung my eyes: my secret shame was now displayed. Just by looking at me, people would know I was different.

I turned towards the glass doors, thinking of flight, of escape from this place where I'd never belong. There, in the cloakroom beyond, I caught a glimpse of pink. Someone was there, someone else like me, hanging up her blazer and hat. I was not alone, not alone, not alone. . . . The relief made me feel slightly giddy.

She walked in, looking lost and bewildered. Like me, she hated coming in to a room full of people. I looked at her, standing there uncertainly in her pink dress, and felt almost fond of her. 'Hello Lindsay,' I said at last. 'I passed,' she said, flatly. 'I have to stay on two more years.' 'Yes,' I replied, 'me too.'

It was the most we had said to each other since the day of her party.

I recognised the wary expression shadowing her hazel eyes. 'I'm glad you've got pink,' I said. 'I thought I was the only one.' She smiled briefly, and we went and

36

found two chairs near the back as the headmistress came into the hall.

As we sat side by side, I watched her long, delicate fingers nervously pleating the skirt of her dress. We hadn't been given a choice, she and I. We hadn't even been consulted. The choice had been made for us, long ago, and there was nothing we could do now to change it. We were different from the others in a way that we would never have chosen. From now on, we would always be pink in a world of yellow and blue.

COMPASSION

A Prayer

One of the things I found hardest to accept during the trauma was my own feeling of helplessness. I was continually on the receiving end, constantly asking other people for help. And no sooner had they given it than I was asking for more: 'Listen to me, explain it to me, tell me what to do now.'

I felt I had nothing to give, nothing worthwhile that I could offer, nothing that I could do for anyone else. This began to undermine my fragile sense of self-worth still further.

Then I read the results of a MORI survey of 2019 adults in Britain: 10% of them had had at least one sexually abusive experience before the age of 16. 'That must be an underestimate,' I said to myself. 'What about people like me who have repressed the memory? If they had asked me, just a short time ago, I would have said no, I have never been abused.'

So I realised that there was something I could do: I could pray for these others who had repressed all memory of their abuse. They were even more helpless than I was: they were still suffering the long-term damage, but did not know the cause and so could not even ask for help.

It was only a little thing, but it was something I could manage, and it was a small movement out of the self-centredness the trauma had pushed me into. It is not possible to do much for anyone else in the midst of a trauma, nor is it a good idea to try. But little things, like writing a prayer, and using it, can help.

The prayer asks for nothing specific, only the ultimate victory of God's love. The vocabulary has been carefully chosen: the word 'father' has been avoided, and the word 'love' used sparingly. These words, and others, can cause difficulties for victims. Those abused by their fathers or a father figure may have trouble relating to God as father; those for whom the abuse was defined as a form of 'love' will find this word, too, hard to accept.

As a result of using this prayer over a period of time, I began to feel compassion for adult survivors of child sexual abuse. I could not feel compassion for myself: I hated and blamed the 'child within' for what she had been involved in, and despised the adult I had become. But expressing compassion for others who had suffered in a similar way was a first step in having compassion for myself and the child I had once been.

JESUS, our brother and friend,
look with kindness and compassion
on those who were sexually abused.
You see the lost child within
still crying alone in the darkness
where the hidden wounds of childhood
still hurt, and make them afraid.
When they feel abandoned, give them hope,
when they feel ashamed, give them comfort,
when they feel unloved, give them faith,
when they feel betrayed, give them peace.
In the power of your resurrection
may love triumph over fear,
light shine in the darkness,
and the long reign of terror be ended.

CONFRONTATION

A Mad Computer

I found it difficult sometimes to look at my situation objectively. I may have known what kind of conflict I was facing, but the feelings and pain associated with it were sometimes too strong for me to be able to sort out the issues clearly. What I needed, at times like that, was a form of communication that made the situation look less frightening and enabled me to step back a little from the reality.

And so I used to find stories that seemed to reflect my situation, and tried to see myself as one of the characters. As I started trying to interact with the other characters, the story often began to take a new course, and provided me with a way of exploring the conflict I was facing. The only requirement for the story to work was that I should be able to identify quite strongly with one of the characters, and see my own situation reflected in theirs.

This approach is rather similar to some of the well-known ways of meditating on gospel stories, and I have done that too, by identifying with the Samaritan woman at the well (John 4) and Jairus' daughter (Mark 5), among others. But I have discovered that other stories can help in a similar way. This is an example of one that I used successfully in order to get to grips with the barriers that prevented me from gaining fuller access to my lost memory.

This happens to be a science fiction story, but I have also used a number of others, including the legends of the Holy Grail, Greek myths and television dramas.

Doing it effectively only requires me to 'let go' and let my imagination take over and take the story where it will, which might be a long way from the original plot. It can be a long process, going on in bits and pieces over several weeks, as this one did. But persevering with it can produce worthwhile results.

Lifting conflicts out of the present and placing them into the realms of science fiction, fantasy, myths or legends, makes them less threatening and can even be very enjoyable.

My memory returned first as a few facts and an emotional storm that could not be neatly identified or named. I felt as if a bomb had gone off, leaving a vast area of devastation and rubble. Chaos reigned for several months: I could not sleep, had trouble eating, and could not do even the most simple, routine jobs. But as that began to subside, I realised that, while I now knew what had happened all those years ago, it was still somehow separated from me as an experience. It was as if all knowledge of the rape had been sealed off in a kind of bubble and kept quite separate from the rest of my life. I now knew what information was within that bubble, in some detail, but I was still unable to get inside it. It was as if there was some kind of 'guardian' around it whose job was to prevent me getting too close. Whenever I tried, the guardian would attempt to drive me out again. I had created this guardian myself in order to protect myself from remembering. It was dangerous to me to remember: my whole world might fall apart. I had tried to speak about the rape, but had been told, in effect, that it had not happened. If something that terrible could happen yet 'not be real', there was something wrong with my perception of reality. Even as a child, I was aware that if that was the case, then I must be insane. Insane people were taken away and locked up; I certainly didn't want that, so I locked the memory up instead and set up a guardian whose job was to prevent me ever remembering. One of the guardian's chief tools was my fear of insanity. This fear would arise if anything reminded me of any aspect of the rape, and I would quickly back off.

The guardian had originally been a form of self-protection, and had done its job well. But over the years, as I grew up, its power grew. It was as if it was 'programmed' to protect the memory at all costs, even at the cost of destroying me, and another of its tools was to make me feel suicidal. This was clearly more dangerous to me than the memory of the rape, and yet the guardian did not seem to realise this. It was faithfully following the instructions it had first been given: don't let me remember. Don't let me even dream about it in ways that might remind me of what happened. But the guardian was beginning to break down. I had remembered the facts, I had been overtaken by some of the deeply buried and devastating feelings. Now I wanted to get into the memory more fully. Things had changed – it was now more dangerous to try to forget than to remember it all.

My father had been a keen reader of Arthur C. Clarke's science fiction stories. He bought all the early books and, at quite a young age, I began to read them too. Even though I could not always follow the story lines, I was fascinated by the atmosphere they evoked, by the possibility of other worlds, where life was different, and strange beings lived. Life was exciting in these worlds, full of danger and the unexpected, but it always worked out all right in the end. They were much more interesting worlds than the one I lived in, dominated by fear and the need to appear as normal as possible. My world was grey and lifeless, and I was only half-alive in it. Arthur Clarke's worlds were bright and colourful, and I escaped into them with relief.

Perhaps it was this early introduction to Arthur Clarke's stories that led me to create a game with a computer based on his later books, *2001: A Space Odyssey* and *2010: Odyssey Two*. The guardian of my memory seemed to me to be very like the computer, HAL, that appears in these stories. HAL was a highly sophisticated computer, with the power to speak, who controlled the spacecraft Discovery on its mission to Jupiter.

Unfortunately, due to a conflict in its basic programming, HAL developed a form of neurosis: the mission had to succeed at all costs, even if this meant destroying its human crew. HAL wiped out the sleeping members of the crew by turning off their life support, and then tricked two other members into activities that caused their deaths. Only one member of the crew remained: Dave Bowman, alone on board the Discovery, cut off from communication with earth, with a computer that could not be trusted controlling all the functions on the spacecraft.

So I imagined myself as Dave Bowman. In order to survive, I had to persuade HAL to release more of my memory, and if possible, convince him that we were both on the same side. I tried to open a dialogue with the guardian by calling it 'HAL':

+ Good morning, HAL.
− Good morning, Dave.
+ HAL, do you remember the song your programmer taught you when he was teaching you to speak?
− 'Daisy, Daisy, give me your answer, do.
  I'm half crazy, all for the love of you.
  It won't be a stylish marriage,
  I can't afford a carriage,
  But you'll look sweet upon the seat
  of a bicycle made for two.'
+ That's great, HAL. I knew that song was in your memory. I knew it, too, when I was a child.
− Is that when you were being programmed, Dave?
+ Something like that. Now, can you search your memory banks and tell me what Daisy's answer was?
− I'll try, Dave. Is this a game?
+ That's right, HAL. There's nothing else to do out

here in outer space, and I'm tired of chess because you always win. I think I can beat you at this game.

The song, 'Daisy, Daisy', which does appear in the Arthur Clarke stories, should put the guardian in touch with the time of the rape. It is a song my father taught me, which we would sing as he walked me to school each morning on his way to work. We had other songs as well, but this was our favourite.

Following this first attempt at dialogue with HAL, I had a violent nightmare. It included images of the rapist's face, terror, darkness and no one to help me. I woke from it in a sweat of terror – rejoicing! It was the first time a dream had shown any aspect of the rape directly. There had been oblique references in dreams since the return of the memory, but nothing like this. The guardian had released something and let my dreaming self approach.

+ Nice move, HAL! That's one point to you. But I think I can outwit your next move.
− I don't understand the rules of this game, Dave.
+ That's part of what you have to find out. I'll tell you the score each time a point is scored, and you'll be able to work it out from that.

HAL won a point for each attack on me that produced an emotional or physical reaction that related to the rape.

Panic attack, violent nausea, abdominal pain, feelings of terror.

− What's my score now, Dave?

+ Five points.
− What's your score?
+ Also five points.
− I think I know how I get points, but I'm not sure
how *you* score.
+ I'm sure you'll work that out quite soon.

The answer is that HAL and Dave were on the same side. When HAL scored a point, so did Dave, as long as Dave understood the connection of the reactions to the rape.

Another nightmare! Lucy Lockett, the nursery-rhyme character, was beheaded. I woke in terror again.

+ Another point, HAL. Well done.

Abdominal pain, insomnia and tension.

+ Two more! You are doing well.
− What are we playing to, Dave?
+ First to reach ten points.

I had another nightmare, also featuring Lucy Lockett, which was almost an exact repeat of a nightmare I had had as a child shortly after the rape. It depicted the rapist as a huge fox with sharp teeth and a lolling tongue. This nightmare had brought my mother into my room asking what was the matter? Had something nasty happened at school? Had someone been unkind to me? She cuddled me and soothed me, and I realised that I was in great danger. I might easily say something about the rape inadvertently, or give her some clue as to what had happened. Nightmares were dangerous – they made me vulnerable. I panicked, and resolved to have no more. Nor did I, though images of a fox or large beast sometimes appeared in less frightening dreams.

+ You're up to eight points now, HAL. For the ninth point, describe Lucy Lockett.
- She had long light-coloured hair, wore a white mob cap, a pink and white dress and pantalettes. She tasted nice, sort of sweet.
+ Do you mean she was the picture on the tin I kept my sweets in?
- She was, but she comes before that.
+ Are you referring to the picture in the nursery-rhyme book?
- That was not in colour. I've described her, so I get the point.

Dave did not get the point, though, as I did not know what HAL was talking about, or how it was related to the rape. I did vaguely recognise the description he had given, though I could not place it.

+ Where is Lucy Lockett, HAL?
- I cannot answer that question.
+ Who is Lucy Lockett, HAL?
- I cannot answer that question.
+ Why can't you answer the questions?
- The answers are not in my memory banks. It must have been before my time.
+ For the final point, which will win you the game, what else can you tell me about Lucy Lockett?

At this point, I was not sure whether the guardian was on my side, giving useful information, or not. It was quite possible that it had tried to divert me onto an apparently irrelevant track. However, I felt that there was a good possibility that Lucy Lockett was somehow connected to the rape since she did appear in my childhood dreams at around that time. And so I decided not to challenge HAL with being obstructive. I would assume for the moment that he was telling the truth when he said that he did not have the answers.

It was at this point that HAL started to produce lists. I could not see the point of them, but his printer was working overtime:

Trespassers Will
Lived under the name of Sanders
The lion and the unicorn
Henry V at Harfleur
St George and the dragon
King John was not a good man
Robin Hood and Maid Marian
Friends and relations
Rabbit
Daffodowndilly
Tattoo was the mother of Pinkle Purr
The table in the nursery
Chrysanthemums, yellow and white
Once upon a time there were three little foxes
Water-lilies
Bonnie Dundee
Lavender's blue, dilly dilly
The archangel Raphael
Angel of God, my guardian dear,
Matthew, Mark, Luke and John
It's a good sort of brake . . .

Was I supposed to accept this as an answer to my question? It didn't seem to have anything to do with what I'd asked. I decided to go on assuming that there was something in it, and examined the list. Some of the items were, I could see, references to the Christopher Robin books by A. A. Milne. That accounted for Trespassers Will, Sanders, King John, Tattoo and quite a few of the others. I had to go out and buy copies of these books since my old ones had long since been given away. I enjoyed it – I hadn't re-read them since I was a child. I found twelve items on the list among their pages. Then I remember another book I had at that time, *The Dragon Book of Verse*. It wasn't a children's book, but I had loved it, and my parents used to read to me from it. There was a drawing of Henry V at Harfleur in it, illustrating a passage from the Shakespeare play, the poem 'Matthew, Mark, Luke and John', also with an illustration, and a poem about Robin Hood. HAL's list, I discovered, was a list of references to books I had had and liked at around the time of the rape. But I couldn't work out how they related to Lucy Lockett, except through my old nursery-rhyme book, which HAL had already discounted.

+ The list is from my children's book, HAL, but I'm not accepting that as enough to win you the point.
– It's the best I can do, Dave. The answer you want is not in my memory banks.

There is little point in losing one's temper with a computer. I had the frustrating feeling that I was close to remembering something important that would give me greater access to the memory. HAL had stopped lashing out at me with panic attacks and abdominal pains. Was he finally on my side? I decided to try to test that out a little.

+ Tell me, HAL, the best question to ask you now, the

one that will bring me closest to what I want to know.
- Why didn't you ask me before, Dave?
+ I'm asking now.
- Ask me, 'Where be dragons?'
+ OK, HAL, where be dragons?
- In the Christopher Robin book, *Now We Are Six*.

I went back to the book again. At least I'd narrowed the field down to one book. I found the poem HAL was referring to. It is called 'Us Two' and describes how Christopher Robin and Pooh find 'dragons'. There was nothing in that poem that seemed to help. Was it elsewhere in the book? HAL had stated the book, not the poem, as the place where the best answer he could give lay. I looked through the rest. At the end of a poem called 'Explained' there was a drawing that made me feel very peculiar: it was of a battered rag doll.

I conceded the game to HAL, but I could go no further at this time. It often happened during the trauma that something would arise, come close to the surface, and then subside again. It was over a year before the question of Lucy Lockett re-emerged, and I found out that HAL had been telling the truth: it was not in his memory banks, but he had come as close as he could to giving me the answer.

HAL reached ten points and won that game, but I was the real winner. The guardian had cooperated with me, and begun to release more of the memory.

CHILD OF GOD

Playing Games

Children use toys not just to amuse themselves, but also as a way of coming to grips with life. They play situations like 'schools' and 'hospitals', using dolls or stuffed animals, and through them they begin to understand the things that happen to them. They may also play 'birthday parties' as a way of prolonging a pleasurable event, or 'weddings' as a way of expressing their ideas about their future. Toys are not simply objects they use, but in some cases actors in the drama, representing other people or the child herself.

Playing with anatomically complete dolls is one way that very young children are helped to describe their experiences of sexual abuse. It is less threatening to tell such a story as if it happened to a doll.

I had many dolls in my childhood, most of which were given away or thrown away at some stage, since they had no particular significance for me. But there were two that I never parted with. They became much more than toys to me because they were linked, in my mind, with the rape.

This section describes one of the ways in which I used them. In this instance, it was to resolve questions concerned with my Christian initiation. This can be a serious issue for sexual abuse victims who come from a religious background: they may feel that the abuse 'disqualified' or 'invalidated' their baptism or other participation in the life of the Church. Since the ceremonies of initiation (baptism, confirmation, first communion) cannot be repeated, it may be necessary to find ways to go back and reclaim them. That is what I used my dolls for. First, I had to understand what they symbolised for me, and then I was able to involve them in a game.

For other people, different games might be appropriate. For example, a doll could be baptised. Or, in some cases, a funeral service might help: grief is a very real part of facing up to sexual abuse in childhood, and the funeral of a doll could be a way of recognising and accepting that grief. Or, if someone believes that her doll represented a part of herself that 'died' as a result of her abuse, perhaps there could be a beatification ceremony that declared her to be among the saints in heaven.

Of course, there are many other issues that playing with dolls might help with; this is just one example of an issue that mine were successful in helping to resolve.

In a photograph taken when I was about seven, I am holding the two dolls shown on the front cover. One is fair-haired, blue-eyed Diana, the other dark-haired, brown-eyed Beverley. In my mind at the time, these two dissimilar dolls were twins, and had to be kept together.

I remember clearly the day the photo was taken. We had just moved to a new house, and my father wanted some pictures to send to my grandmother. He asked me to come out onto the back porch. I panicked. I used to like posing for him, and from the earliest time I could remember, his old Brownie camera had seemed like part of his face. My expression in those early photos is open, trusting and relaxed. I looked directly at the camera with eyes wide open, smiling. But by the time he wanted to take this picture, things had changed. I had a terrible secret, something I had to keep hidden from him, which I was afraid the camera might reveal.

There was no escape, and so I rushed into my bedroom, where things still lay in boxes, and grabbed the two dolls. I could hide behind them, at least partly. There was a low wall around the porch, and I stood the two dolls on it in front of me. I hoped they would help to divert his attention. My expression in this photograph is guarded and wary, very unlike earlier ones. I was nervous, too, fiddling with a shirt button, which betrays my inner fears. I had learned, also, how to put my eyes out of focus if anyone looked at me directly. That was what I was doing as he pressed the shutter button.

The photo is framed now and hangs on my wall. I have given it a place in my life, for the story it tells is not one that needs to be hidden any longer. There is nothing to be afraid of any more, nothing to hide, and nothing so terrible that it cannot be brought out into the light.

The two dolls are here, too, side by side in an arm-chair. Unlike my other dolls and toys, I never passed them on to my younger sister. There was something important about them, some reason why I must never let them go. When I got too old for dolls, I packed them up in a box and put it into the attic of my parents' house among the packing cases and trunks filled with other people's mementoes of the past. But if ever I went up into the attic for any reason, I would always unwrap them and look at them, and wonder why it was I still felt I had to keep them.

Four years ago, I went up into the attic and fetched them. I brought them home and sat them on the armchair, though I had no idea why I wanted them. As a child, I had liked Diana, and played with her a lot. I had not liked Beverley, and was even a little afraid of her. I found that I still did not like Beverley, and whenever I picked her up, I had a tendency to shake her quite roughly.

They sat on the chair for five months, and then Beverley, whose mouth had always been firmly shut, began to 'speak'. What she had to say was not something I wanted to hear. She knew about the rape; she had always known, and now she was telling me about it and there was no way to stop her. I realised then that, after the rape, the dolls had changed from toys into symbols, and that was why I had always kept them and regarded them as twins. They were two parts of one story, two parts of me. Diana was the good girl who knew nothing about the rape. She was my conscious self, deliberately unaware of what had happened and, on the surface at least, not noticeably different from other children. Beverley was the bad girl. She knew all about it, though her lips were sealed. I never played with her much, and locked her away in the toy cup-board as often as I could. Yet I could not afford to lose her: some vital part of myself would be lost with her, a part I had disowned but might one day want to reclaim.

As symbols, the dolls have proved very helpful. They have enabled me to play and act out various conflicts. Within weeks of the return of my memory, as the first emotional storm it unleashed began to subside, I found I had a terrible conflict around the issue of whether or not I was really a Christian. I wanted to be, but I discovered an underlying fear that, because of the rape, I had forfeited any right to belong to the Church. So I had to go back and look at the ceremonies of my Christian initiation.

My first step was to visit the church where I had been baptised. It was a Church of England parish church where the names of all who have been baptised there are inscribed in gold letters on wooden plaques. I saw that my name really was there. Then I took out the family album that had photographs of the event. I was just a few months old, and wore the family christening robe. I was also able to find my original certificate which carried the text, 'Suffer the little children to come unto me', which seemed particularly appropriate. The godmother who had carried me to the font was still alive, so I was able to ask her about the ceremony. She remembered it very clearly, right down to the family argument about the choice of godparents for this first member of the new generation.

All this helped to convince me that the ceremony had really taken place, but having discovered that I really had been baptised, I immediately became convinced that, in some way, the baptism must have been invalid. Even though the Roman Catholic Church had later accepted it, and not re-baptised me even conditionally, I was quite sure that there must have been something that they had not been aware of at the time. As I investigated this feeling, I discovered that I had an erroneous view of what baptism was, and that the logic behind it was the logic of a child, and ran backwards: I had been raped later – God had not protected me – I had been taught that God protects his children – therefore I was not one of his children – baptism makes you a child of God – therefore I was not validly baptised.

In investigating this conflict (and others), it was as if I was two people: the adult I am today, and the child I was. I had to learn to listen to the child within me, take her seriously, accept her feelings and encourage her to tell me what she thought, even though it might sound very silly to me now. By doing this, the issue became clearer, and provided me with a way of resolving it.

First, though, I needed some re-education in the theology of baptism. I read books, listened to tapes, and asked a priest for instruction. It took quite a time for me to come to understand that baptism does not mean that God will protect us from all harm and suffering, and thus that the rape was not a sign that he had rejected or abandoned me. On the contrary, the lives of the apostles, saints and martyrs show that suffering is part of life, including a Christian life, and everyone experiences suffering in some form or another. The difference that baptism makes is in revealing that suffering has meaning and value, and is not, as it appears, simply meaningless destruction. Christian suffering is a participation in the sufferings of Christ; it is thus a journey towards wholeness, towards resurrection and the new life promised by the Gospel. It is a journey towards God, not away from him, and is a dimension of human life in which God is with us, even when we are totally unaware of it. He is present just as he was present when Jesus cried out, 'Why have you abandoned me?'

Although, on an adult level, I was gradually able to

come to understand what baptism means, and what it does not mean, this new understanding meant little to the child within me. Somehow, I had to find a way to bring it down to her level, so that she too would accept the validity of her baptism.

By listening to the child within me, I discovered that there was a symbol of the invalidity she was sure existed: my pure white garment, the symbol of the innocence and purity of the newly baptised, had not been pure white. I had worn the family christening robe, a lacy affair that was traditonally threaded with pink ribbons for a girl and blue for a boy. Those pink ribbons, which defiled the pure white, had become symbolic of my fear that my baptism must have been invalid.

I was able to get the robe and examine it. In doing so, I discovered that it had a separate full-length petticoat. This petticoat was pure white, right down to its buttons and tapes. 'There you are,' I told my 'child', 'other people may go to heaven in their lacy dresses, but you can go in this petticoat.' It was a solution that the 'child' found very satisfactory.

The fear of invalidity recurred at times, though never with the same intensity, and used to express itself through the differences between a Church of England baptism ceremony and a Roman Catholic one; for example, 'I did not have a candle' or 'I was not anointed'. One priest to whom I explained this, told me that I could regard my baptism as being rather like an emergency baptism. He told me that there was a recognised form of 'supplying the ceremonies' for babies who had been baptised in hospital because they were thought to be in danger of death. Together, we adapted and informally celebrated the relevant aspects of this service, and the fear has not reappeared since then.

But, having dealt with this problem, another one

quickly arose. At the time I was received into the Roman Catholic Church, confirmed and made my first communion, all memory of the rape had been repressed. So now I felt that part of me had been left outside the church door, and that perhaps the Church would not have accepted me had the rape been known. I knew that this fear was irrational and had no basis in reality, but nonetheless, it was very real to me, and I needed to do something to combat it.

Symbolically, it seemed to me that Diana, the good girl, had become a Catholic, while Beverley, the bad girl, had been left outside. I had been received into the Church using an early form of the Rite of Christian Initiation of Adults, which has now been adopted as the normal rite for receiving adults into full communion. At that time, though, only a provisonal form had been available, and that was what had been used for me. I was able to find a copy of it, and it seemed to me that I needed to bring Beverley into the Church in the same way through a 'play' ceremony.

Before my own reception, I had made my first confession. I decided that, prior to Beverley's reception, I needed to re-make that confession in the light of the new view of my past that the return of the memory had brought. There was no difficulty in doing that: I took Beverley with me, having first explained to the priest what she symbolised and why it was that I wanted to make a general confession, looking back at the whole of my life. The priest I chose to go to was someone I knew well and whom I had already told about the rape some weeks previously. So I had no fears about how my confession would be received. I knew I would be treated kindly and sympathetically.

When this had been done, I made Beverley a new, white dress for the occasion, and started deciding how it was to be enacted. Although it was to be a play ceremony, roughly on a par with a doll's tea party, I wanted someone who really was a priest to be there and receive Beverley. My own role, I had already decided, was that of Beverley's sponsor, someone who is already a full member of the Church and stands with the candidate, much as a godparent does at a baptism. In Beverley's case, I would also have to speak for her as she could not speak for herself.

I had a friend who was a priest, but I felt a little shy about asking if he would come and play a game with me and my doll. However, I plucked up my courage, and was pleasantly surprised by the interest he showed and his willingness to take part. I set up a spare room to resemble the church in which I had been received, and I discovered that my friend's interest was genuine when he arrived at the appointed time, bringing a bedspread to represent liturgical vestments, and his teddy bear to join the congregation.

We went through the rite as if Beverley was a real person, but dumb, and the questions were put in the third person. For example, he asked, 'What does Beverley ask of the Church?' rather than 'What do you ask. . . ?' And so Beverley was confirmed and received into full communion. I hoped it would be a real communion that would unite the lost part with the rest of me.

In working through the trauma that the return of my memory induced, I often found that it helped to let myself become a child again, and do the things that children do in order to understand the world around them. The success of this particular game was not immediately apparent. The process of healing is long and slow, and it took almost two years for a new symbol to emerge that would reveal that this game had indeed been successful in uniting 'Diana' and 'Beverley'.

POWERLESSNESS

A Drawing

Sometimes, as I worked through the trauma, I would come across something that I could not put into words. It was usually directly concerned with the way I experienced the rape. I would be aware of it only as some kind of feeling, a sort of nebulous dark cloud to which I could attach no words. These were the feelings of the child I had been, for which my vocabulary at the time had been inadequate. Trying to apply words I had learned later did not help: they meant nothing to the child within me, who was still caught up in the emotional experience of the past.

I once worked in a kindergarten for a few weeks. One of my tasks was to set out the paints and paper for the art period. I used to watch the teacher going round asking the children about their paintings: 'Is this your house? Who is this person? And what is Mummy doing? Is this you helping Mummy?' Then she would summarise what the child had told her, and write a caption on the bottom: 'Mummy and Vanessa make cakes for tea'. Even before the children had learned to read, they were learning how words could be used to express their ideas and feelings.

When I found myself blocked, unable to express myself verbally, I gave the child within me some large sheets of paper and a set of coloured felt-tipped pens. I can't draw, but I drew as children do, with no concern for artistic merit. My first drawings tended to be abstract designs in violent colours. I recognised orange and red as anger, dark jagged shapes as pain,

61

deep green as hatred, and the overall design as a reflection of my confusion over what was happening to me.

Later, I drew a picture of the rape itself, then one of a nightmare. Still later, I began to draw cartoon strips because I realised that, at the time of the rape, I had had little concept of the idea that events were consequential on each other. I needed to help the 'child' place events into the order in which they had happened, and so bring some sense of order into her confusion.

This is one of the drawings I did. I waited until I had finished it before I began to ask myself questions about it. It revealed the powerlessness I had experienced in the rape, a powerlessness that was first physical and then more pervasive, making me unable to extricate myself from the long-term consequences.

What does the drawing show? A little girl falling backwards over a precipice.

What does falling backwards mean? It was a game we used to play in the school playground before it was forbidden: one of us would stand with arms outstretched, and fall backwards, letting a partner catch her. If you didn't move your feet as you fell, you won. If you did, your partner won. But there is no one to catch the little girl in this drawing. She trusted someone to take care of her, and instead she got hurt. So this shows 'breakdown of trust'.

Why is there no colour in this drawing? Because colour means life and vitality There is no life here, it has all drained away. The tree shows life and growth, but it is left behind. The little girl's life has changed forever; she can never get back to where she was before. This feeling is called 'desolation'.

Why has the little girl got no face? Because she doesn't feel like a person any more. She doesn't know who she is. This is 'loss of all sense of identity'.

Where will the little girl land at the end of her fall? Nowhere. She will go on falling forever. She is falling into nothingness, oblivion. This is called 'despair'.

Is that little girl me? She is Beverley, my rag doll. She has got Beverley's shoes on.

This kind of self-questioning helped a lot in clarifying my feelings and telling me how I had, in fact, experienced the rape. I had not known the word 'rape', or even the concept, and my sexual knowledge at the time had been limited to knowing where babies came from. So I didn't understand it as a sexual attack, because the concept was totally foreign to me. As this drawing shows, the devastation caused by the betrayal of trust, and an intuitive awareness that nothing could ever be the same again, were two aspects of the way it seemed to me at the time.

There was one consistent feature of my drawings that it took a long time to understand: I invariably drew myself in the form of a rag doll. Picture after picture showed me either as Beverley or as some other rag doll, never as myself. I knew there must be a reason for this, but I could not discover what it was.

When I picked Beverley up one day, I noticed the way she flopped. Her head and limbs all flopped backwards. If I shook her, she flopped about. She couldn't stand or sit on her own: she had to be propped up in the armchair, very unlike her plastic twin who could sit and stand unaided. Beverley's flopping fascinated me. I even dropped her a few times to see how she would land – always with her arms and legs spread-eagled, and her head on one side. I began to feel that I was a rag doll with floppy arms and legs. I started letting my head flop about like hers to see what it felt like.

And then I knew the answer: I drew myself as a rag doll because I had felt like a rag doll. As I was attacked, I went totally limp. I remembered the terrifying feeling of being unable to make any part of my body move. I was powerless against the rapist, a rag doll in his hands.

And then I was overwhelmed with a sudden surge of guilt. The rape had been all my fault. I should have run way, or screamed, or tried to fight him off. But I did one of those things – I just went limp. The rape was wrong, evil, and I had let it happen. So I was an accomplice in the evil that had been committed. It was my fault that it had happened: I should at least have tried to stop it. Now I knew why it was that I hated myself so much. I was an evil, wicked child who had let something terrible happen.

It didn't seem to me that going limp was a normal, human reaction. Flight or fight were supposed to be the instinctive responses of anyone, even an animal, to the recognition of danger or threat. Going limp was not normal, therefore I was not normal. There was something fundamentally wrong with me, with my instinctive reactions, and my will to survive. I had let it happen; I had consented to the rape.

At the time of the rape, I was going to a Catholic primary school. In our library periods, one of the younger Sisters used to read us stories about saints. Maria Goretti had been canonised just a short time before, and perhaps it was because she was a child saint that Sister chose to read to us about her.

It was the story of a girl of twelve, pestered by a neighbour who, finding Maria alone one day, attempted to rape her at knife-point. Maria fought back, saying 'No! It is a sin', but the man was stronger than she was. He did not succeed in the rape attempt, but Maria died, defending her virtue. And then the Church canonised her, and declared her to be a saint.

It simply validated my conclusions: the Church, too, was saying that I should have fought back, even if it meant being killed in the attempt. The Church, too, seemed to be saying that I was guilty of the rape.

The issue that I had to deal with here was that of my powerlessness. I had to accept that I had been a child, powerless against an attack by an adult. I had to accept, too, that I was powerless to control my instinctive feelings and reactions. My reaction had been to go limp, and I was powerless to choose any other. For a long time I felt that my body had betrayed me by acting in this way, until I discovered that 'freeze' is a normal and recognised response by victims of violent crime. But my feeings of guilt, self-blame and complicity took a long time to disappear.

Continual reassurances from friends that it had not been my fault, and that I had not consented, acted like gentle drops of water that wear away a stone. I was helped, too, by new books on child sexual abuse that talked about the way children blame themselves: at least I wasn't the only one. Perhaps I wasn't so abnormal after all. I went out into parks and shopping areas and looked at the size of children in relation to the adults around them: how vulnerable they are, how small. They wouldn't stand a chance in an attack by an adult.

There was nothing wrong with my instincts, or my will to survive. Going limp is a survival strategy once you accept that you are powerless. Every muscle in my body was made loose and relaxed. I was as soft and pliable as a rag doll. The sudden pain was searing, blinding and sharp, but much less than it would have been had my body been tense and tight.

Last year, on the feast of St Maria Goretti, I gave a short talk. It meant I had to go back to her story and take a fresh look at it. This is part of what I said on that occasion.

'Today we are celebrating the feast day of a victim of child sexual assault. Faced with rape, Maria Goretti found the power to say no, though at the cost of her life. . . . Not all children faced with sexual assault

66

have the power to say no, nor to make that no effective, even if they say it. As a result, some of them find the story of Maria Goretti very distressing. They believe that, by canonising her, the Church is telling them that they ought to have had that power, that they ought to have fought back, even at the cost of their lives. Because they couldn't, or didn't, they suffer from a deep-seated guilt, a form of survivor guilt.

But the story of Maria's life and death can be seen in a different light: that here is a victim who, though reduced to the total powerlessness of death, ultimately triumphed over her abuser, and left him powerless against her. He killed her, but did not destroy her, and that, I believe, is an important aspect of the message the Church is giving by canonising her – that through the grace of God, the weak triumph over the strong, the powerless over the powerful. Every victim of child sexual abuse, or any kind of abuse of power, is like a grain of wheat that falls to the ground. But it is in the victim's powerlessness that the grace of God can act, whether that powerlessness is total, as in Maria's death, or partial, as in those of us who survive. It is the Easter message of the triumph of the victim, the revelation that the power of resurrection is at work, both in our death and in our life. And that makes Maria Goretti a source of hope and encouragement for victims of all kinds: our powerlessness, whatever form it may take, is the ground into which the grain falls, from which new life can rise.'

THE PAST MADE PRESENT

Making a Doll

Dealing with something that happened a long time ago can be difficult. Although I found that I remembered the rape itself in great detail, right down to the clothes I was wearing and what the weather was like, the passage of time had made many other aspects of my life at that time rather hazy.

In trying to re-create a fuller picture of my life then, in order to see the rape in context, I found various ways of 'going back to the past'. I visited the place where we had lived, I asked older people what they remembered of that time, and I looked at family photograph albums. All this helped me to build up a more complete picture.

But what no one could tell me, and no photograph could reveal, were my feelings and perceptions at the time: no one could tell me what the rape had been like 'from the inside'.

Trying to go back to the past would not help me with that, for I could not truly roll away the intervening years and re-enter the situation as an adult. The child I had been was no longer in the place where we had lived, nor in photographs. The only place where she could be found was within me. And so I needed to find a way to 'bring the past into the present', and bring her forward in time so that her perceptions and feelings could become part of my adult self.

A way of doing that came about almost accidentally: there had been a doll I had lost. What would happen if I re-created that doll and made her 'appear' again in the present, as fresh and bright as she had been on the day she had first been given to me?

The essence of this exercise is not simply to find an old toy or something else one had at the time, for whatever it is, the passage of time will have changed its appearance. The objective is to re-create something in the present so that it appears now as it was then. It might be a doll or soft toy, a cot blanket (made to be the same size in relation to one's body as it had been in childhood) or an item of clothing (made to fit the adult). It needs to be something to which there was a strong attachment at the time, and which has some association with the experience of sexual abuse.

Lucy Lockett lost her pocket, Kitty Fisher found it.
There was not a penny in it, but a ribbon round it.

'How can anyone lose a pocket?' I had asked my mother, puzzled.

'It was an old-fashioned pocket,' she explained. 'It was separate from the dress, like a small cloth bag or purse. Women wore them hung from a belt or sash. Don't you remember the picture in the old nursery-rhyme book, the one with Lucy Lockett wearing a dress with pantalettes, and Kitty Fisher holding up a small bag? That's what a pocket is.'

Yes, I remembered the nursery-rhyme book. It had been my mother's, and from the earliest time I could remember, she had read them to me and pointed out the pictures that went with each rhyme. There had been a few coloured plates in it on shiny paper, but most were small line drawings set beside the text. Lucy Lockett and Kitty Fisher had been one of these drawings, one that I had liked.

More than thirty years after that conversation, I was walking through the haberdashery department of John Lewis's on Oxford Street. Suddenly, I was rooted to the spot, staring fixedly – but at what? I felt the beginnings of terror: I wanted to run out of the shop, out into the open, but I could not move. I was frozen.

'Stay calm,' I told myself. 'This has something to do with the rape. I am perfectly safe really. Breathe deeply and slowly. What is it here that has reminded me of the rape?' The breathing exercise helped to calm me down. In the two years since the rape memory had returned, I had learned how to cope with apparently irrational attacks of terror. They might happen anywhere: at home or in the street, when I was alone or when I was with people. There was never any warning. But I had discovered also that they were not usually irrational: they were a response to something that had suddenly reminded me of the rape. Very often, it turned out to be a smell. Or a glimpse of someone who looked like the rapist. Or the tone of someone's voice, or a phrase they had used that reminded me of him. Or someone might have touched me, even accidentally, in a particular way, and I would feel the imprint of their hands burning on my skin for hours afterwards.

Quite often I could defuse a terror attack if I could find out what had triggered it. As the deep breathing started to calm me, I searched around for the cause. I used all my senses: no one had touched me; I could not identify any disturbing smells; there was no strange taste in my mouth; I couldn't remember having heard any sounds or voices that upset me. So it must have been something I'd seen. I looked all around me, but all I could see were ranks of embroidery silks and buttons. On the far wall were boxed tapestry sets. Was it a picture on one of those? The answer proved to be no. So it must have been something I'd walked past just before I felt the terror. I went back to the entrance to the department, and retraced my path. Suddenly, my stomach lurched. Right in front of me was a rack that held plastic faces for rag dolls.

I took one off the rack. Hadn't I once had a doll like that, a rag doll with a plastic face? No, I decided. The face didn't smell right.

What an extraordinary thing to think: 'The face didn't smell right'! What was it supposed to smell like? Well, I told myself, it smelled like my doll, Diana. She was plastic, but not this sort of plastic, and it smelled different. It smelled like . . . what? . . . Well more like celluloid. And it was more brittle, too. In fact, that was why . . . and Lucy Lockett lost her pocket . . .

I bought the face. Then I went to the fabrics department, bought a yard of calico, the old-fashioned kind that has stiffener in it, a yard of plain white cotton, some white lace, half a yard of a printed cotton dress material, and some bright orange tapestry wool.

Within 48 hours, I had made a rag doll. Her body was calico, and her hair was bright orange in two plaits. She wore a white mob cap, pantalettes edged with lace, and a cotton dress with a sash.

I had worked in a frenzy, not really knowing what I was doing, but able to ask myself at times, 'Is this what she was like? Does this look right?' and knowing whether the answer was yes or no. I went to make some tea when she was almost finished. In the kitchen, I got a flash: there had been a rag doll with orange hair, half as tall as me, which I'd needed two hands to pick up.

No, I told myself, I'm thinking of my old doll, Gertrude. She had an embroidered face.

Yes, something cried out, but why did she have an embroidered face? Only because the plastic one broke, and couldn't be replaced!

And I remembered. The first doll I had ever had, which I had loved devotedly, was a rag doll called Lucy Lockett. No one except me knew that that was her name, for I was too young to speak. She had been dressed like the drawing in the book, and the similarities had been pointed out to me: 'Look, she had a mob cap, just like your doll, and pantalettes too.' I had had no concept of naming things: if these similarities existed, then the doll wasn't simply *named* Lucy Lockett, she *was* Lucy Lockett.

I had taken her everywhere with me, and had her in my bed at night. I used to suck her hands: they tasted slightly sweet. Then, one day, Lucy's celluloid face broke. I took her to my mother who had always been able to mend her when her arms and legs fell off. But this time, she couldn't mend her. Instead, she embroidered a face. She handed the doll back to me – and my world fell apart. This wasn't my Lucy: it was some other doll. My father christened it 'Gertrude', and I accepted this new identity. I played with it, since I had no other dolls, but I grieved for Lucy and didn't understand where she had gone.

There are no photographs of me with the doll as she originally had been, but there is one of me with my mother and the doll with the embroidered face. I was nineteen months old when the picture was taken. The doll was half as tall as me, and I had needed both hands in order to hold it.

Now my long-lost Lucy had come back. She looked right, she felt right, she even tasted right. I named her 'Lucy Too'.

But what did she have to do with the rape? I'd had dreams and nightmares about her, and in my game with HAL the computer over a year before, she had been the answer to a question. But if she was the answer, what was the question?

For two years I had known all about the rape: when, where, how, what happened right before and right after. But one question I could not answer was 'How did I understand it at the time? What did I think was happening?' It was this question that Lucy Too answered, for within her the two parts of myself were once again united. She combined my two later dolls, Diana, the good girl who didn't know about it, and Beverley, the dark one, who did. Like Diana, she had blue eyes and smelled of plastic; like Beverley, she was a floppy rag doll. Lucy was the child who had been split into these two parts by the rape. She had first existed in the innocence of babyhood; now she had returned in a new body, and taken the two separated parts back into herself.

Lucy had been lost and forgotten years before the rape. And yet, in that moment of anguish and terror, I had remembered her. There was no escape from the rapist, yet somehow I had managed to 'escape': it was as if I was somewhere else, watching from afar. The rapist was the devil, with horns and a tail, twenty feet tall, large and powerful. And he had something in his grip: he had my Lucy. I wanted to scream, 'Give her back! She's mine!' but there was nothing I could do. To save myself, I had vanished from the scene, and I couldn't get back to rescue her. The devil chopped off her arms and legs, and ran her through with his long, sharp claw. Blood spilled from the wound on her back, and I knew that Lucy was dying.

She was mine, but I had forgotten her and left her behind. He had got her, and killed her, and her death was all my fault.

That was how I perceived the rape at the time. I went into a state of disociation where 'I' seemed to be in a different, safer, place, leaving my body behind.

A JOURNEY OF DISCOVERY

Going Back to the Past

Journeys are a symbol as old as mankind. Sometimes life itself is spoken of as a journey. The history of the people of God begins with Abraham setting out on a journey, leaving the security of his home in Ur for an unknown future (Genesis 12).

Pilgrimages are symbolic journeys, a microcosm of the journey of life. They first became popular in medieval times when pilgrims would leave their normal, everyday life and set off on an adventurous expedition to a holy place or shrine. In those days, the journey could be full of peril and danger. The objective of the pilgrimage was not simply to reach the shrine, but to bring something back, such as a palm or shell, and thus the ultimate goal of these journeys was to return home. The person who returned was not quite the same as the one who had set out. He had had adventures, overcome dangers, and seen new places and people. He had grown as a person.

During the trauma, I made a number of symbolic journeys. Some, like a trip of Lourdes, were pilgrimages in the traditional sense (though these days the perils of the journey are usually confined to being delayed at an airport). But I made other journeys, too, which are less overtly religious but equally symbolic.

This section describes one of those journeys. I went, like all true pilgrims, to find something and bring it back. I found more than I expected to, and returned home changed: I had grown in my knowledge of myself and in my ability to accept the truth.

Making a symbolic journey or pilgrimage need not be a long or expensive process. I did this one in less than a day. I found that the important thing was to know why I was going and what I hoped to find. Sometimes I would return believing that I had not found anything, and that the journey had been useless. But another important element is to spend time later reflecting on it. And when I did that, I would often find that, though I had not found what I thought I was looking for, I had found something else instead.

Setting out on a journey expresses a willingness to explore and discover new things. Working through the trauma of child sexual abuse is like a journey itself: it means leaving one's normal life on one side for a time, and exploring and discovering the issues. In the process, one is changed. In the end, one becomes a new person, the one who has faced all these things and overcome them.

When my memory first came back, a deep flood of relief and release broke in on me. I felt light, as if I had put down a burden I had not known I was carrying. I felt almost normal again after the panic attacks and flu-like symptoms of the previous few weeks, and I looked at the memory with wonder: so that was what it was. That was what had gone wrong all those years ago. Of course it was, and I had always known, but could not bring myself to look at it before.

This sense of well-being and restoration lasted for about two hours. Then, suddenly a 'voice' broke in: 'You're making it up!' And the peace was shattered. Was I making it up? Was it real? I no longer knew. Was it, perhaps, just a nightmare I had had, or a fantasy I had made up? Wasn't it Freud who said that children made up things like that as a normal part of growing up? So who was I to dispute with Freud and say that this was anything but normal?

At that point, I almost let the memory go again, but I was aware of a 'child' in distress, a child all alone with no one to help her, hidden deep within me. Didn't I owe her something, having ignored her all these years, and refused even to acknowledge her existence? Didn't she have a right to be listened to, at least, even if I could not believe her?

I got out a notebook and pen. I would see what it looked like on paper. But what should I write down? Was it true or was I making it up? Well, I would write it as it seemed at that moment, with all the confusion around it. I picked up the pen and wrote: 'This goes way back . . . and I have an internal censor that says it isn't true, and perhaps it isn't. My mother told me never to go with strangers, but he wasn't a stranger. I have these images in my mind, and this is what they mean . . .' I described them, and explained them, continually

77

fighting off the censor, and ending up with the words, 'I find this very hard to believe.'

As I read it through, I was overwhelmed with peace again, but again it didn't last. I needed to tell someone, to find out how it sounded to someone else, someone who would be honest with me. I had always found it difficult to trust people, but I did know one person, a priest, whom I felt I could tell. I phoned and arranged to meet him. Then I panicked: I'd never be able to say it, not say it aloud. So I sealed my written account in an envelope, marked 'please read this before I come', and sent it to him.

I did not say, at that time, that it was rape, for although I knew it, I had not put that part into words yet, even for myself. I said I had been molested. He was kind; he listened; he believed me. That was enough just then: he believed me. He did not say that it didn't matter, nor that it was all a long time ago, and above all, he didn't blame me. He simply believed me, believed that it was possible, that it might well have happened exactly as I had said.

Again there was relief; again it did not last. But now I had a friend who knew, and was on my side. No one had ever been on my side, on the side of that little girl, before. And what had happened to me mattered: it mattered to him because it mattered to me. I mattered, and that gave me strength.

But it all seemed so unreal, as if it could not possibly have happened. Surely no one we had known would do a thing like that? Surely things like that don't happen to people like me? Ours was a respectable, respected family: surely, it could not be true.

It seemed to me then that even the town we had lived in, where the rape had happened, was a figment of my imagination and could not be a real place. Why, I had imagined it all: our house, my school, the park and the shops, and the place where he had taken me, the place where it had happened. Yes, that was it: they were all figments of my imagination.

I got out my book of road maps. The town was listed in the index. I turned to the map, and there it was, marked. Well, all right, the place was real, but I had never lived there.

It was not very far away. I would be able to drive there and back in a day. So that was what I decided to do, to find out if I had ever lived there.

Early the following morning, I set off, equipped with a flask of tea, sandwiches and a camera. I felt like an explorer going to an unknown place where the natives could not be trusted to be friendly.

As I approached the town along the main road, I began to recognise things: gravel pits, a church spire, the name of a small village nearby. I had not been back since we moved away, but I certainly knew this place. Some things had changed: there was a new bypass and an industrial estate I did not know, as well as areas of new housing. But I could still pick out many features that I remembered.

I stopped in the town centre. The old High Street had been turned into a pedestrian precinct, but Woolworths was still in the same place, and the old clock tower. The natives were friendly enough, and I bought a street map, which I pondered over a cup of coffee. I could remember what our address had been (it had been drummed into me, in case I ever got lost), but not where it was in relation to the town centre. All I could remember was that we'd had to take a bus to get into the town.

I was terrified that the house would not exist any more, and that the street might have been redeveloped.

But as I drove into our street, I realised that very little had changed. The house was there. It had some new, double-glazed windows, but it was the house I knew. I had lived there. I could remember that. I parked the car and walked to the house, and noticed the front garden wall – it was the same one. I bent down to touch it, and the roughness of the curved top felt totally familiar. I wanted to go inside and look round, but I did not have the courage to go up and ring the bell.

A bus stopped not far away. Two elderly women got off. 'Excuse me,' I said, 'but do you live near here? Do you know where the Catholic primary school is?' One of them did, and gave me directions, so I set off to retrace my old walk to school. It was further than I had expected, and at first, nothing looked familiar. 'It can't have changed all that much,' I told myself; 'these houses are all quite old. Why don't I remember it?' 'Because you are too high up,' a small voice in my head said. 'Look down, at the level a child would be at.' I did, and yes – there were those strange low walls I had always wanted to go and jump over; there were the railings I used to run my hands along; there was the garden where there used to be two tortoises. And, finally, there was my school: not the big concrete and glass buildings that dominated the site, but the brick building at the side, with an asphalt playground beside it. I could remember the face of my teacher, and the names of girls in my class, and how my blue shoebag had hung from the cloakroom peg.

So the house was real, and the school, and I had really lived here. But what about the place where the rape had happened: a field beside a lane, with a hedge? I had no idea where to begin looking for it. I realised that it might have been built over. Perhaps one of those new housing areas now covered it, or the new secondary school I'd noticed. I marked every place on the map that looked like a possibility, and drove to each in turn. I knew it had not been very far from the house, so the range of possibilities was limited. There were plenty of country lanes, plenty of fields and plenty of hedges. How would I know the right place, even if I stumbled across it?

I parked the car on a verge at the beginning of a lane at the fourth site I visited, and began to walk down it, remembering, this time, to look down at a child's level. The lane was narrow, and had been tarmacked. 'That's new,' I said to myself, without realising the implication. 'It used to be a dirt lane with tyre tracks in it. Some of them were deep, and had muddy puddles in them.' I walked for about ten minutes. Well, it could be the place: there was a lane, a hedge and a field, but there must be hundreds of such places. I walked on a little further, then decided to go back to the car.

I turned: I was seized with terror. All my bones felt like water. My hands and feet tingled and went numb. I gasped for breath as if there was a heavy weight on my chest. My hip joints began to hurt. Sharp, sudden abdonimal pains started to stab at me. It was deep, deep inside me – pain, scratching and burning. Blood – I had forgotten the blood. This was the place, for my terror was still here, waiting for me, like a dark but invisible cloud surrounding it. But was it the place? Could I prove it to myself? Yes: as I turned round in the lane, I had seen again the distant block of flats that overlooked the field. I had seen that once before. I had seen it during the rape.

I fled back to the car, not knowing how I got there, and locked myself in. Shakily, I lit a cigarette: I had found what I was looking for. As I started to calm down, I poured some tea from my flask, and decided it was time to go home. There was no need to look any further: it had happened, and it had happened here.

The shortest route back to the main road went past our house. There was a car in the drive that had not been there before, and through the window of the upstairs bedroom, I could see a man on a step-ladder. I found I now desperately wanted to see inside the house. At least I could ask: they could always say no.

I turned the car around and went back. I walked up to the door, and rang the bell. It did not sound right: it must be a new one. What on earth was I going to say? I was still upset from my experience in the lane. Surely it would show, and I'd be dismissed as a crank.

A grey-haired man answered the door. It was the man I had seen on the step-ladder.

'Excuse me,' I said, 'but I used to live here as a child.' I didn't know what else to say.

'Oh, I see,' he said, as if he did. 'I expect you'd like to look round, then. Did you have the small bedroom at the front?' It was not quite what I had been expecting him to say. I'd been trying to think up some way to prove that I really had lived there.

'No,' I replied. 'That was my brother's. I had the one at the back.'

We went round together from room to room. Although everything had been modernised, I could remember how it had been. I started to tell him: 'The coffee table was here, the armchairs were over there, the radio was on a shelf on that wall. . . .' Then I realised that this might be rather boring; after all, this was his house now. 'No,' he said, 'go on. I'm interested in the history of the house.' So in each room I described where the furniture and fittings had been. I was amazed at how much I could remember.

Upstairs, he apologised for the mess. He was redecorating. The fitted carpet in the main bedroom had been taken up. 'Oh!' I said, rather too loudly. 'What is it?' he asked. 'The floorboards,' I replied. 'The staining round the edge. I remember my father putting that stain on.' I remembered it vividly: I could even smell the liquid he'd used. This was quite definitely *our* house.

As we walked down the upstairs corridor, I suddenly stood stock still and felt very sick. I had heard a voice, the thoughts of a child, a child I knew very well. It came back in all its freshness, as if it had only just been thought. In this exact same spot, more than thirty years before, I had stood there and suddenly thought: 'I wonder if that means I'm going to have a baby? I shall have to tell Mummy.' I'd been trying to understand the rape.

By going back to find these places, I had been exposing my memories to the reality of a house, a school, a town and a real geographical place. I believed that, if they were fantasies, they would fade away in the face of reality, much as a dream that seems very real, fades away on waking. Instead, the reality confirmed my memory, helping further details to emerge. And I learned that the memory was not only in my mind – it was in my body too. Physical sensations connected with the rape had returned as I stood in the lane. My body confirmed what my mind had, at times, doubted.

Yet despite all this validation, I still found it hard to believe. And this persisted for almost three years, especially in times of stress. But as a result of this journey of discovery, I learned to call it by its real name: it was not 'doubt' but 'denial', an unwillingness to accept the truth. I did not want to believe it could have happened, for that made the world a very unsafe place.

The denial went away whenever I felt safe, and returned whenever I did not. But very slowly, over time, the periods of denial got weaker and shorter. I asked the child within me once how she had coped when she had tried to speak about the rape and had not been believed. She said, 'I told myself it didn't happen.' 'In that case,' I said, with my adult superiority, 'can you say now "I told myself it didn't happen, but it did"?' 'That's silly,' she replied, with that disconcerting directness children sometimes have. 'You don't bother to tell yourself something didn't happen unless it did.'

AWAKENING

Re-education

Awakening to a new realisation of God's presence and activity during the trauma did not happen all at once. It was a gradual process, during which I started to un-cover false ideas about God, misconceptions about the Gospel and gaps in my understanding. They had al-ways been there, and I had lived with them without being aware of how negatively they affected my views of myself, God, the world and the Church.

As they rose to the surface, I realised that I needed to re-educate myself. I read books, joined a tape library, went to lectures and took courses. These did not just deal with religious subjects, but also with things like assertiveness, creative self-expression, and surviving child sexual abuse. After each of them, I tried to set down on paper what I had learned. Sometimes it was little or nothing. Other times, it was a lot. This section is an example of one of these 'evaluations'. I wrote a letter to the instructor of a course on St Paul in which I expressed what I felt I had learned from his lectures.

Re-education in all kinds of areas can be very help-ful, not just in gaining knowledge and understanding, but in improving one's self-image. A course in pottery, embroidery, microwave cookery or self-defence can give a sense of achievement, competence and self-worth, as well as providing a welcome form of relaxa-tion. There was only one rule I made for myself about taking courses or classes: if it does not help, or makes things worse, then stop. It may simply not be the right time to try.

Dear Professor,

At the end of the course evaluation form you handed out at the end of term, there was a section that asked, 'Are there any other comments you would like to make about this course (the teachings of St Paul)?' Mine won't fit on the four lines provided, so I hope you will excuse me submitting them on a separate sheet.

The last time I studied St Paul was more than twenty years ago, when I was taking Scripture A level. He caused me tremendous problems, probably because of the way he was presented to me. As a victim of child rape, I often seem to interpret things differently from other people. In addition, I was quite young at the time, and so I was approaching the texts with the rather literal mentality of an adolescent.

One of my worst problems came from 1 Corinthians 6:15–16:

Do you not know that your bodies are members of Christ? Shall I therefore take the members of Christ and make them members of a prostitute? Never! Do you not know that he who joins himself to a prostitute becomes one body with her? For, as it is written, 'The two shall become one'.

From this, and what the teacher and commentary said, I believed that St Paul meant that I was 'one body' with the rapist, forever, and there was nothing that could be done about it. In other words, I was cut off from the body of Christ. Unfortunately, Romans was not on the syllabus, or I would have realised that the 'one body' bond would dissolve at death at least, and thus was not eternal (Romans 7:1–6).

The other major problem came, more predictably,

from passages like Ephesians 6:1, 'Children, obey your parents in the Lord, for this is right.' There are passages in other letters that make the same point. I tried to obey my parents, but they did not understand the effects of sexual abuse, and of course, they had not believed me when I had tried to tell them about the rape. Thus much of what they told me to do, 'for my own good', placed an intolerable burden on me. I needed all my strength just to cope with life; having additional demands made as well was more than I could take. The regime of obeying my parents, being told to look after my younger brother and sister, and that as the eldest, I was responsible for helping in the house, with the shopping, and substituting for my parents in their absence, contributed to my anxiety and depression. It was hard enough just to look after myself. I believed that St Paul was telling me that I had to put up with this state of things. Because of my negative view of myself, I came to believe that that was the way God wanted me to be treated, and hence I had a completely false idea of God. It built up over time – this idea that the Christian life was one of continual humiliation, of being crushed and kept in a state of guilt and subjection. I tried my best, but found it so intolerable that I rejected God and became an atheist, and refused to attend school prayers any longer.

There were, too, passages in St Paul that I loved, especially the long and beautiful meditation on love in 1 Corinthians 13, but they were painful to read because I thought he had already said that these things weren't for me. Having come up with a completely false view of what Paul's version of the Gospel is, it was reinforced by passages like Galatians 1:6–7:

I am astonished that you are so quickly deserting him

who called you in the grace of Christ and turning to a different gospel – not that there is another gospel. . . .

I took this to mean that what I understood of Paul's gospel was the one and only interpretation that was possible.

Since to me the rapist was the devil (and had appeared in my dreams as such), and since I had been on picnics with him with my family, from 1 Corinthians 10:21–22, I believed that I could never complete my Christian initiation and make my first communion. The text says,

You cannot drink the cup of the Lord and the cup of demons. You cannot partake of the table of the Lord and the table of demons. Shall we provoke the Lord to jealousy? Are we stronger than he?

So I expected terrible retribution to follow any attempt to 'partake of the table of the Lord'.

So to say that St Paul caused me problems at school was putting it rather mildly.

For me, then, it was Paul himself who created the veil that made the Gospel impenetrable (2 Corinthians 4:3, 'And even if our gospel is veiled, it is veiled only to those who are perishing'), and I was unable to see anything but this false version of the Gospel whenever I read the synoptic Gospels, which were also part of the A level course. Luckily, John's Gospel was not on the syllabus, so my conversion from atheism, when it came, clung onto that and the other Johannine writings.

But, eventually, one has to come to terms with St Paul. I went on a retreat a year ago, determined to tear the veil that obscured the Gospel. I was sure, by then, that my interpretation, and that of my scripture teacher, was wrong, but I did not know how to correct it. What was the real Gospel of St Paul?

My retreat director gave me a list of passages that he described as 'the heart of St Paul'. They included Romans 5:2–11, and 8:14–39; 2 Corinthians 5:1–21 and Ephesians 2—3. I tried to read them as if I had never seen them before. And the veil began to dissolve.

> And *you* he made alive, when you were dead through the trespasses and sins in which you once walked, following the course of this world, following the prince of the power of the air, the spirit that is now at work in the sons of disobedience. Among these we *all* once lived in the passions of our flesh, following the desires of body and mind, and so we were by nature children of wrath, *like the rest of mankind*. But God, who is rich in mercy, *out of the great love with which he loved us*, even when we were dead through our trespasses, made us alive together with Christ (by grace you have been saved) and raised us up with him. . . . (Eph 2:1–6 – my emphasis).

I began to realise that I was no different from anyone else: we are all affected by sin in one way or another, and we are unable to get out of it on our own. The good news that Paul has to bring is that God has reconciled the whole sinful world to himself. And that includes me.

So I was making some progress in the right direction, and I even wrote a brief summary of how I understood the message of these passages I was reading:

> We are acceptable to God because he has accepted us; not because we are good, but because *he* is.

It was then that I found that one of the other retreatants

had a taped lecture on St Paul, one given by you some time ago. I borrowed it, and found that you were reinforcing my new understanding. I couldn't grasp everything you were saying, but I knew then that I wanted to hear more of your interpretation.

It took me a long time to organise things so that I could attend one of your courses on St Paul. In fact, when I enrolled, I was a little afraid in case I had misunderstood the tape and you would tell me that my original understanding had been correct. I did, after all, get the A level, and with a fairly good grade.

Your course, though, has served to strengthen and reinforce my new vision, and set me off on new lines of thought and study that I shall continue to pursue. I found the course liberating, challenging, exciting, fun. . . . I'm sorry I burst out laughing in class quite so often. You must have thought it was rather odd. It was simply my expression of delight every time you knocked down one of my false assumptions. I can't yet formulate all that I have learned, but I can give you just one example of the liberation your lectures provided.

Let me digress for just a moment to fill you in on the background: I have never had trouble reading the Old Testament. I don't mean that I always understand it, because I don't, but I mean that it never upset me. It reflected the image of the God of my experience. At school, in the second year, we girls in the scripture class were the envy of the rest of our year, because in scripture lessons words like 'adultery', 'fornication', 'whore', 'harlotry' and, of course, 'rape' had to be explained to us. (This was long before the biology mistress got round to reproduction in mammals, which was to be the basis for our sex education.) The passages we were studying, which required us to know the meanings of these words, showed me a God who was totally familiar with the use

90

and abuse of sex, and accepted that it was a part of human experience. Not a desirable part, but something that happened, something that he knew all about, something that did not have to be hidden from *him*, even if it did have to be hidden from other people. After all, 'this is the word of the Lord'.

I had not recognised that one of my problems with the New Testament came from the fact that I could not find rape or sexual abuse mentioned in it. There are no rape victims in the healing miracle stories, no teaching on what to do if you were one, and so on. I began to think that Jesus, unlike the Old Testament God, hadn't known about these things. He knew about prostitution and adultery, but he didn't seem to know about rape. Nor did any of the New Testament writers.

It was the lectures on Paul's letter to Philemon that gave me the breakthrough here: the story of the runaway slave, Onesimus, whom Paul baptised. Paul took Onesimus' debt to Philemon on himself, perhaps as a way of showing how God takes our debts and sins on himself, and then reminded Philemon of the unrepayable debt he himself owed Paul: the gift of eternal life in Christ, brought to him by Paul's preaching. So, confident that Philemon will now forgive the debt, since he cannot in all conscience demand repayment from Paul, Onesimus is sent back 'no longer as a slave but more than a slave, as a beloved brother' (verse 16). In the course of these lectures, you gave some explanation of what slavery was in Paul's time: not just work with no payment, but the training of men, women and children to perform certain sexual acts for their masters. Sexual abuse of slaves, you said, was common, expected, and simply part of their lives. They had no rights, even over their own bodies. I didn't laugh at this revelation – I nearly fell off my chair. I had found where sexual abuse was in the New Testament: within the concept of slavery. Thus, whenever slaves or slavery are mentioned, sexual abuse is included. Now the New Testament has something to say to me; I know where I fit in.

I see now that I was wrong in saying that the 'other comments' I would like to make can't be confined to the small space given on the form. I think I can summarise them, so perhaps you would complete it for me. In the relevant section, please write just this: 'with love and thanks, Onesimus'. It will fit the space you provided.

PROTECTION

An Answerphone

The trauma was so severe at times that I had to find ways and means of protecting myself. There were days when I could not think straight, my eyes blurred and my hands shook so badly that I could only ever fill a mug of coffee half full. But I could not afford to cut myself off from the outside world entirely: life had to go on.

One of the ways I protected myself was to get an answerphone. This meant that anyone could phone me at any time, but I could choose my own times, when things were a little calmer, to return calls. By leaving the volume turned up, I could find out who was phoning and what they wanted, so it also enabled me to screen calls.

It was a defence, and I needed defences. Apart from the answerphone, I had other, less technological ones: like becoming hostile so as to drive people away, or withdrawn and uncommunicative so as to put them off.

But there were people who knew how to get through my defences: they acknowledged my right to protect myself and my right to privacy, but they were not put off. They offered nothing but friendship and caring, putting no pressures on me, but simply continuing to 'be there'. Because of that, I would let them through, and welcome the support they offered.

I never actually left this message on the tape, but there were many days when I would have liked to.

It is important to have defences, for facing up to

childhood sexual abuse makes victims very vulnerable. People who mean well can do or say the wrong things and make the situation worse. Having defences is not a cop-out: it is a way of beginning to take control of one's life, rather than being simply a victim of circumstances.

Click. 'Hello, this is Tracy Hansen. I'm afraid I'm not able to take your call at the moment. In fact, I'm sorry you've phoned right now, because I'm in the middle of some kind of crisis. This is one of my bad days, and I don't want to talk to you or anyone else. You can leave a message on the tape if you really must, but don't hold your breath waiting for me to call you back. Whatever it is you want, I can't cope with it today.

If you're calling about something related to work, well, all I can do is offer you my condolences. I'm not going to do any work today. I can't. I don't dare to speak to you because I can't put words together in any way that makes any sense. And I can't type a simple sentence without making three errors at least. So whatever it is I am doing for you, if it is something that requires a brain or hand and eye coordination, then I'm afraid you're right out of luck.

If, on the other hand, you are a member of my family, then I just want to say that I hate you all. I didn't yesterday, and perhaps I won't tomorrow, but today I do. If one of you has given birth, announced an engagement or got divorced, just send me the information on a postcard. If it's anything less important, then please go away.

If you're the man who is supposed to be coming to install the bathroom heater, forget it. Icy cold bathrooms fit my mood perfectly, so I think I'll do without one. I can't sit in the bath feeling sorry for myself if the room is glowing with warmth. It just doesn't have the same satisfaction.

If you are the bookshop to say that the new book on sexual abuse I ordered has arrived, well I'm not interested. I don't want to read what anyone else has to say on the subject. I know it all already. It's no consolation at all to know that I'm not the only one who has been through this. As far as I'm concerned at the moment, I *am* the only one, so you can send the book back.

I think that covers just about everyone who might phone today. If you're someone I haven't thought of, I'm sure you'll get the message too.' Beeeeeeeeeep.

'Hi, Tracy, it's me. Are you hiding behind the answerphone again? That's OK. I just phoned to see how you are. I know you have the volume turned up, so you can hear what I'm saying. Well, take care of yourself, and I'll phone again in a . . .'

I intercepted that call. I'd forgotten that I had friends. It can be quite infuriating, when you've convinced yourself that no one cares, to find out that someone does. In fact, it can completely ruin an otherwise perfect Bad Day.

HEALING RITUALS

A Dance

I cannot explain exactly how, or why, healing rituals work for me. In this section, I talk about three that I have used frequently. Two of them are part of the official liturgy of the Catholic Church. The third is one I made up for myself in order to try and understand more fully what the Church's liturgy was telling me about the rape. In effect, the liturgy was 're-naming' it, telling me that the rape was not the senseless act of destruction it appeared to be, but had the potential to become a sharing in the Passion of Christ. It would then have meaning and value, and its ultimate outcome would not be death but the beginning of new life.

In my ritual, I tried to bring together the events of my experience and those of the Passion, binding them into a whole, enabling me to see the rape in a different perspective.

I found that in many ways, I felt unconnected to the world around me; one of the ways I could feel more connected was to walk barefoot, feeling the texture of the ground beneath my feet. And sometimes I can express my feelings more easily in movement than in words. As a child, I had weekly ballet lessons that taught me a sense of rhythm and music, and gave me an ability to express myself in this way.

These are two elements of my ritual, for basically it is a dance, done barefoot. The overall objective is to create the form of a cross contained within a circle, but along the way, and between the dances, I have 'stations' where I pause and reflect.

I perform this ritual in a field near my home. To get over the embarrassment of being observed, I go out very early, before sunrise. This adds a new dimension, for the dance begins in darkness and ends in full daylight.

However, I also do it on a smaller scale at home, using buttons to mark the stations and ribbons to create the figure. I find this also works, though it is not as satisfying.

The ritual could be adapted quite easily: each station can be replaced, and different topics and texts chosen. For some stations I have several alternatives. There is nothing 'magical' about this form of it – it is simply an aid to prayer that involves mind and body working in harmony.

The Catholic Church has two sacraments that directly involve healing: the sacrament of reconciliation, and the sacrament of the sick. I had not thought of the sacrament of reconciliation (often referred to as 'Confession') as a healing sacrament until this aspect of it was explained to me. I had thought of it only in terms of forgiveness, and thus the only things I thought that I should speak about were things I regarded as my own personal sins. But once the trauma began, I had trouble deciding what was and what was not my fault. Then the healing aspect was explained to me, and I began to use the sacrament differently: usually, I divided my confession into two areas, very roughly (and they often overlapped). First, there was the area of personal sin, and secondly there was the area of things that I knew were not my fault, but needed healing. And so I would mention them, sometimes in general terms, and sometimes in more detail. I also invented a third area: sometimes I was aware of 'something' but had not been able to put any words to it, so at the end of whatever else I wanted to say, I would ask for a short time of silence, 'for when we cannot choose words in order to pray properly, the Spirit himself expresses our plea in a way that could never be put into words' (Romans 8:26). I would ask the Spirit to pray in me, bringing to light whatever lay hidden which I was only vaguely aware of. I often found that, during the week that followed, I would become aware of what it was that was still hidden, and then I would mention it explicitly in my next confession.

The sacrament of the sick, which used to be used only for people in danger of dying, is also one that I have relied on heavily at times. Nowadays, it can be used for any serious illness, and healing from past sexual abuse can certainly be serious in that sense. I have had many crises when I was only aware that I was in great emotional pain and reaching a deep level of desperation in which I was tempted to give up on everything. At times like that, I found the sacrament of the sick very helpful. For one thing, it made me aware that sexual abuse was something that needed healing and was a serious matter. It made me feel that *I* mattered, and that what was happening to me mattered as well. But also, I was asking Christ to come into my situation, to make my suffering part of his own, which issues in new life rather than destruction. Frequently, there was no noticeable improvement after I had received the sacrament; sometimes things even got worse! But always there was the inner assurance that, despite all appearances to the contrary (and they usually were to the contrary), 'everything was ultimately all right'.

In order to understand more fully what these two sacraments meant in terms of my own experience, I made up various prayers and activities of my own. On its own, suffering, and especially innocent suffering, is meaningless; united to the sufferings of Christ, however, it is revealed as having value. Its value for me includes bringing me into a new relationship with God, who revealed himself first not as the creator but as the one who led his people out of slavery in Egypt. The rape was an evil that put me into a position very like slavery, a position of being oppressed and unfree. But it is from this position that I am able to come to know God as the one who leads people into freedom, and is true to his promise to deliver us from all evil.

This ritual is a prayer-activity that I find particularly helpful. It involves creating the form of a symbol – a cross contained within a circle. This symbol is associated with wholeness, and with the centre of one's being. The psychologist Carl Jung noticed that young children who had been hurt tended to produce this symbol, or variations of it, in their drawings.[1] It is also one of the oldest symbols known to mankind. I found that it was appearing in my mind just before my memory returned, and that if I doodled, especially while talking on the phone, I would find that the doodle contained it.

I perform this ritual in a field of longish grass, because that will show the imprint of my feet, and that is how I make the symbol itself. I use twelve stones (white, round ones that I collected from a beach) to mark each of the stations along the way, and I call the ritual 'The Hours of the Cross'. It is, in some ways, similar to the more traditional 'Stations of the Cross' since it is an alternative form of meditation on the meaning of the Passion in relation to my own life.

'The Hours of the Cross'

The first hour: the rape

First, I put down one of the stones to mark the spot. Then I call the rape to mind, and reflect on this text from the *Epistle of Privy Counsel*, chapter 2:

> Take good, gracious God just as he is, and without further ado lay him on your sick self just as you are, for all the world as if he were a poultice! Or to put it in other words, lift up your sick self just as you are, and through your longing strive to touch good, gracious God just as he is. Touching him is eternal health, which is the point of the story of the woman in the Gospel who said, . . . 'If I touch but the hem of his

101

garment, I shall be whole'. Much more will you be made whole of your sickness through this marvellous heavenly touch. For you are touching his very being, his own dear self.[2]

The second hour: the return of the memory

I put down the second stone on the ground, a little further along than the first, so that they lie on the arc of a circle. Then I recall the return of my memory of the rape, and reflect on this text from the *Cloud of Unknowing*, chapter 6:

> Therefore, I will leave on one side everything I can think, and choose for my love that thing which I cannot think! Why? Because he may well be loved, but not thought. By love he can be caught and held, but by thinking never.[2]

The third hour: a dance

It was the third hour when they crucified him (Mark 15:26).

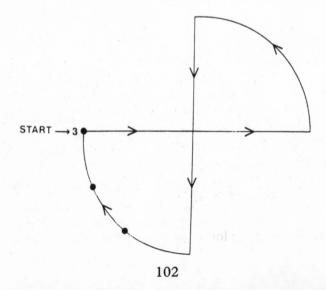

This station does not involve meditation but action. I put down the third stone so that the three are lying as a quarter circle, then walk or dance the pattern shown above in the grass. While I am doing this, I sing the hymn 'Laudato sii'.[3]

The fourth hour: St Francis

St Francis has always been one of my favourite saints, perhaps because of his childlike qualities of simplicity and joy. I put down the fourth stone, and reflect briefly on him, sometimes reciting something he wrote or said. Francis gave up everything in order to follow the Gospel, and so I reflect on that using this text:

> This is only what sanctified common sense would expect: that God should keep safe all who for love of him forsake themselves, indifferent to their own welfare. Small wonder then that they are marvellously kept, who are completely humble in their courageous, strong love. (*Epistle of Privy Counsel*, chapter 6).[2]

The fifth hour: St Clare

As the woman who knew and loved Francis best, St Clare also has a special place in my affections. She was a virgin saint, and so it might seem odd that I, as a rape victim, chose to include her. But I did so for her writing on the subject of religious virginity, showing that it is something that comes from a relationship with Christ, not simply a physical state. In a letter to Agnes of Prague (also a virgin), St Clare included this quotation from the Office of St Agnes:

> When you have loved him, you are chaste,

if you embrace him, you will become more pure,
as you receive him in you, you are a virgin.[4]

And then I reflect on these words from the *Cloud of
Unknowing* chapter 75:

For it is not what you are or have been that God looks
at with his merciful eyes, but what you would be.[2]

The sixth hour: a dance
*From the sixth hour there was darkness over the land until
the ninth hour (Matthew 27:45).*

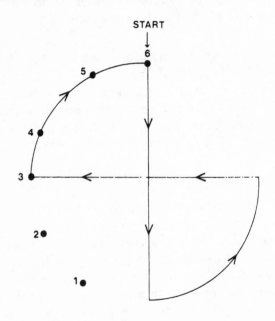

This is another 'action' station, in which I make the second part of the symbol, again by walking or dancing through it. I accompany this movement with the hymn 'Lord of the Dance'.[5]

The seventh hour: the good thief

At this station, I try to see the link between my experience and that of the good thief, who said, 'Jesus, remember me when you come into your kingdom.' This is the station at which I remember the darkest of dark times in my life, and try to see the crucifixion as the darkest time in Jesus' life, and in the history of the world, when the powers of evil seemed to have triumphed. I imagine myself on my own cross, beside Jesus on his, and try to hear him saying these words from Jeremiah (8:18–22):

> Sorrow overtakes me,
> my heart fails me.
> Listen, the cry of the daughter of my people
> sounds throughout the land . . .
> 'The harvest is over, summer at an end,
> and we have not been saved!'
> The wound of the daughter of my people
> wounds me too,
> all looks dark to me, terror grips me.
> Is there not balm in Gilead any more?
> Is there no doctor there?
> Then why does it make no progress,
> this cure of the daughter of my people?

The eighth hour: Mary Magdalene

There is a saying that the darkest hour is the hour before the dawn. At this station, I think of Mary

Magdalene on Easter Sunday morning: surely that was her darkest hour as she set out to go to the tomb where her beloved Lord's body lay. There is no text for this station: I simply spend some time praying for all those for whom this is the darkest hour of their life, for whatever reason.

The ninth hour: a dance
At the ninth hour, Jesus cried out (Mark 15:34).

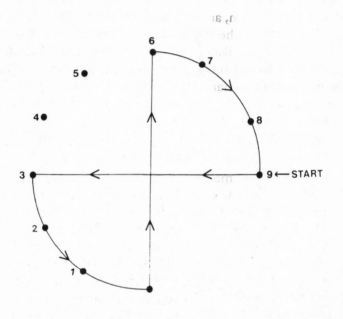

Although the symbol has now been completely formed, the dance is not yet over. At the ninth station, I go back over the path of the third station, but in the reverse direction, binding stations 1 and 2 (the rape and the return of the memory) with stations 7 and 8 (the crucifixion and the burial of Jesus). The song I use for this dance is the carol, 'Tomorrow shall be my dancing day'.[6]

The tenth hour: the harrowing of hell

When Jesus died, so the First Letter of St Peter tells us, he went down into hell, in order to take the word to the 'spirits in prison' (1 Peter 4:18–19). Hell is a place I am quite familiar with, and so I chose this way of describing the meaning of the resurrection as part of this ritual. The text I use is taken from an old homily that is part of the Office of Readings for Holy Saturday. In it, the writer imagines what Christ said there to Adam, whose disobedience had brought sin and death into the world:

AWAKE, O sleeper, and arise from the dead, and Christ shall give you light. I am your God, who for your sake became your son, who for you and your descendants now speak and command with authority those in prison: Come forth, and those in darkness: Have light, and those who sleep: Rise. I command you: Awake, sleeper, I have not made you to be held a prisoner in the underworld. Arise from the dead; I am the life of the dead. Arise, O man, work of my hands, arise, you who were fashioned in my image. Rise, let us go hence; for you in me and I in you, together we are one undivided person.[7]

The eleventh hour: a covenant of peace

Here, I reflect on the promises God has made to us that one day we will reach a place of peace where every tear will be wiped away. There are several texts I use for this station, including the Canticle of Daniel and Hosea 2, but my favourite comes from the Song of Songs, 2:10–13.

My Beloved speaks and says to me:
'Arise, my love, my fair one, and come away;
for lo, the winter is past, the rain is over and gone.
The flowers appear on the earth,
the time of singing has come
and the voice of the turtledove
is heard in our land.
The fig tree puts forth its figs,
and the vines are in blossom;
they give forth fragrance.
Arise, my love, my fair one,
and come away.'

The twelfth hour: a dance

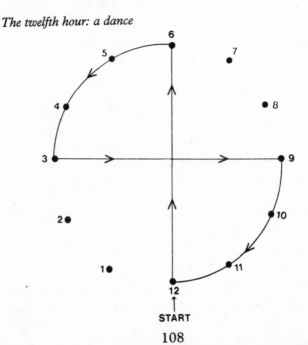

At this station, I remake the part of the symbol I made at Station 6, but going in the reverse direction. The song I usually use is the children's hymn 'One more step'.[8]

The symbol is now complete on the ground, traced out by the movement of my feet. When I have completed the twelve stations, I go into the centre and ponder the text from St John that gave me the idea for 'The Hours of the Cross':

Are there not twelve hours in a day? A person can walk in the daytime without stumbling because she has the light of this world to see by; but if she walks at night, she stumbles, because there is no light to guide her (John 11: 9–10).

THE FUTURE

A Dream

I sometimes have dreams that convey important messages to me. There is one I have had all my life, or at least as long as I can remember. In it, I walk into a room full of familiar people. It is a living room, and they are sitting on comfortable chairs and sofas, in a semi-circle round a fire. I am standing in a doorway – they have not seen me yet. Some of these people are members of my family, others are old friends. It is a comfortable, cosy scene, with friendly talk going on. But I am going to say something that will change everything for ever. I do not know if the change will be for better or for worse. I walk forward, and some of them look up at me, unsuspecting. I open my mouth, but no words come. I wake up, confused and troubled.

Many times during my life, I have thought that I had found that room in reality, but there was always something that was not quite right about it. I kept looking for that room and those people, because what I wanted to say was something that had to be said, even though I could not remember what it was. I felt that if I found it in reality, I would also find the words I needed.

After I spoke about the rape, when I had told several friends and one member of my family, I had another dream.

In it, I walked into a room full of familiar people. They were sitting on comfortable chairs and sofas, in a semi-circle around a fire. I was standing in the doorway, looking at them. Some were members of my family, others were old friends. One of them looked up and saw

110

me. 'Oh good', he said, standing up. 'We've been waiting for you. We won't be coming back again, so we want to say goodbye.' He took me by the arm and led me round the group. Each person in turn stood up, shook my hand and wished me well, and then left the room. Finally, my escort smiled at me, bowed, and left.

The dream has not returned since then. I believe that its purpose was to remind me from time to time that there was something very important I needed to say. Since it had been a life-long companion, I was touched by the way it came back to say goodbye, and did not simply stop occurring.

What I had to say was, indeed, something that changes everything for ever, for my whole view of myself, my family and friends, the world and God has altered radically. I can no longer live in a fantasy world where things like child rape do not happen, or where, if something terrible does happen, someone can wave a magic wand and make everything all right. Now I have to live in the real world where such things can and do happen, and happen to people like me.

Is it for better or for worse? Despite the long period of trauma that followed the return of my memory, it is, I am convinced, for the better. There have been casualities along the way, especially in the form of relationships that did not survive the revelation of the rape, and people who, quite simply, could not cope with what I had to say, and turned away. The cost has been high in some ways.

But all along, I was being set free from the effects of the past. From being locked in a world of fear and emotional isolation, I began to be able to trust again, to form deeper relationships in which I was able to give more of my real self, and to find that life includes enjoyment and happiness as well as pain.

111

The destructive patterns of behaviour that I formed as a result of the rape, and the survival strategies I employed to protect myself from a world that I perceived as hostile and uncaring, have begun to melt away. New patterns, new and more positive ways of living, have started to emerge. I have, in effect, been given a future, one that is no longer primarily determined by the effects of the past, but in which I have the freedom to make new choices and find new ways.

As long as the past still determined my life, the rapist continued to have power over me: the power to frighten me with unnamed terrors, the power to make me keep silent, and the power to exert a destructive effect on every aspect of my life.

The purpose of facing up to the rape and all the issues it raised, and still raises, is to make the rapist powerless against me. My terrors have been named, and now I can understand and assess them in a realistic light. My silence has been broken, and in place of the condemnation I feared, I found loving acceptance and compassion. I now know the origin of many of my problems, and knowing that, I can find ways to change.

In the Lord's Prayer, we say 'forgive us our trespasses as we forgive those who trespass against us.' An alternative translation of the original Greek is 'cancel our debts as we also have cancelled those of people who are in debt to us'. The idea of forgiveness as the voluntary cancellation of a debt is also found in the parable of the unforgiving debtor (Matthew 18:23–25).

It is this concept of forgiveness that makes sense to me. I cannot accept any idea of forgiveness that includes excusing the rape, or implicitly condoning it, or saying, in effect, that it does not matter. To say that it does not matter would be equivalent to saying that *I* do not matter. And there is never any excuse for an adult

112

who takes advantage of the vulnerability and trust of a child in order to abuse her. The severe and lasting effects of sexual abuse have been well documented by researchers. It is not a minor event that can be glossed over or dismissed.

But to see forgiveness as the cancellation of a debt is an approach that I found helpful, for it does not imply that the debt never existed, nor that it does not matter, nor that it was not rightly owed in the first place. All it implies is giving up a rightful claim to repayment.

It took me a long time to reach a point where I was prepared to give up all claims against the rapist. At various times there were different things that I hoped to be able to exact from him, one way or another: an admission of guilt and responsibility, an explanation, an apology, an assurance that it could never happen again, a validation that my memory was accurate, a recognition of the harm he had caused me, evidence of remorse, his conversion, his eternal damnation, a large financial settlement for damages, and so on.

It took an even longer time to realise that as long as I still wanted something from him, however well-justified that desire might be, I was still bound to him. And that no matter what I might be able to obtain, it would not truly compensate for what he had taken from me. I came to see that 'cancelling the debt' was the only way to break the hold he still had on me and become truly free of him.

If a magician were to appear now and offer to wave his magic wand and eradicate the rape and all its after-effects from my life, I would refuse. These years of working through the trauma have been the most valuable of my life: through them I have learned that the new life promised by the Gospel is a reality made accessible to us. The Gospel is for desperate people, those who have no other hope, and the rape placed me among them, the people whom Jesus called 'the poor'. 'Blessed are those who mourn,' he said, 'they shall be comforted' (Matthew 5:4). One retreat director put that into different words for me: 'Blessed are you who experience a crucifixion in your life. You will share deeply in the life of the risen Christ.' The cross is the way towards resurrection, and there is no other way. But the way of the cross, whatever its form, is also the way of coming into a new and experiential relationship with Christ the Redeemer. It is God who leads his people from slavery to freedom and from death to new life; the work of liberation and healing is his work, accomplished in Jesus.

In the desecrated field of the rape, a treasure lay deeply buried. It is the treasure of the opportunity to experience the love of the God who heals his children.

NOTES

Healing Rituals: A Dance

1 Carl G. Jung, *Man and his Symbols* (Aldus Books 1964, reprinted 1974), pp. 165–6.
2 Clifton Wolters (translator), *The Cloud of Unknowing and Other Works* (Penguin 1961).
3 No. 527 (words by Damian Lundy from St Francis of Assisi) in *Celebration Hymnal* (Mayhew McCrimmon Ltd 1984).
4 Quotation from the First Letter of St Clare to Blessed Agnes of Prague, translated by Brian Purfield OFM.
5 No. 131 (by Sydney Carter) in *Celebration Hymnal*.
6 No. 43 (traditional) in Elizabeth Poston (editor), *The Pengiun Book of Christmas Carols* (Penguin Books 1965).
7 *The Divine Office II Lent and Easter* (Collins 1974, 1976), p. 321.
8 No. 188 (by Sydney Carter) in Peter Horrobin and Greg Leavers (compilers), *Junior Praise* (Marshall Pickering 1986).

Biblical quotations throughout the book (except for those on p ii, 99, 105 and 109, which are from or based on the Jerusalem Bible) are taken from the Revised Standard Version of the Bible, copyrighted 1946, 1952, © 1971, 1973 by the Division of Christian Education of the National Council of the Churches of Christ in the USA.

BOOKS

I would recommend:

Deirdre Walsh and Rosemary Liddy, *Surviving Sexual Abuse* (Attic Press Dublin 1989).

Ouaine Bain and Maureen Sanders, *Out in the Open: A guide for young people who have been sexually abused* (Virago 1990).

Sylvia Fraser, *My Father's House: A memoir of incest and healing* (Virago 1989).

Liz Hall and Siobhan Lloyd, *Surviving Child Sexual Abuse: A handbook for helping women challenge their past* (The Falmer Press 1989).

Ellen Bass and Laura Davis, *The Courage to Heal: A guide for women survivors of child sexual abuse* (Heinemann, 1991).

I have found all these books helpful in different ways. For an overall view of the subject and the problems involved, I would recommend above all *Surviving Sexual Abuse* by Deirdre Walsh and Rosemary Liddy (see above). In just sixty-four pages, they cover all the main issues, working from the experience of the Dublin Rape Crisis Centre. It is an excellent introduction for anyone who might find themselves trying to help a victim of childhood sexual abuse, and is a good source of information for people who simply want to know more about what is involved.

For other survivors, I would recommend *Courage to Heal* by Ellen Bass and Laura Davis (see above). This extremely comprehensive book covers every conceivable aspect of the healing process, is sensible, practical and down-to-earth.